Basic Legal Research Workbook

Fifth Edition

ASPEN COURSEBOOK SERIES

Basic Legal Research Workbook

Fifth Edition

Amy E. Sloan

Associate Dean for Academic Affairs and Professor of Law
University of Baltimore School of Law

Steven D. Schwinn

Associate Professor of Law
The John Marshall Law School

John D. Edwards

Associate Dean for Information Resources and Technology;
Director, Law Library; and Professor of Law
Drake University Law School

Wolters Kluwer

About Wolters Kluwer Legal & Regulatory US

Wolters Kluwer Legal & Regulatory US delivers expert content and solutions in the areas of law, corporate compliance, health compliance, reimbursement, and legal education. Its practical solutions help customers successfully navigate the demands of a changing environment to drive their daily activities, enhance decision quality and inspire confident outcomes.

Serving customers worldwide, its legal and regulatory portfolio includes products under the Aspen Publishers, CCH Incorporated, Kluwer Law International, ftwilliam.com and MediRegs names. They are regarded as exceptional and trusted resources for general legal and practice-specific knowledge, compliance and risk management, dynamic workflow solutions, and expert commentary.

This book is dedicated in memory of the Honorable Philip Townsend Cole,
who always emphasized the importance of accurate research.

Contents

Preface

The fifth edition of *Basic Legal Research Workbook* is substantially revised from earlier editions. All exercises can now be completed online (with the exception of one introductory assignment). If print research is no longer being taught or access to print materials is limited, you can still complete virtually every exercise. Although the text is now oriented around online research, some portions can still be completed in print. Accordingly, the text retains its flexibility for a research curriculum that incorporates print research. Specific changes in the fifth edition include the following:

- New organization—Most chapters still contain three exercises, with two exercises focused on step-by-step instruction and one allowing for more open research. The exercises with step-by-step instructions are no longer divided between print and online instruction. Instead, the content has been reorganized to focus on specific sources or skills, and the questions have been formulated so that all exercises except Exercise 1.1 can be done online. Some exercises—specifically, in Chapter 3 (Secondary Source Research), Chapter 4 (Case Research), Chapter 6 (Statutory Research), Chapter 8 (Federal Administrative Law Research), and Chapter 10 (Research Planning)—retain components that can be, but do not have to be, completed in print.
- Updated problem sets—The problem sets have been updated to reflect the new organization of the text and the current functionality of online services.
- Learning outcomes and student assessment—The fifth edition is structured to support student assessment, as required by new ABA requirements. Goals for each exercise have been restated as Learning Outcomes. The Workbook's guided exercises may be useful for formative assessment, while the unguided exercises can be used for summative assessment.
- Online research—The exercises have been updated to reflect the latest versions of Westlaw and Lexis. Questions introducing students to Bloomberg Law and the latest government websites (e.g., govinfo.gov) are also included.
- Print research problem sets—For those exercises that can be completed in print, the total number of problem sets has been increased from 15 to 18, with the flexibility for you to assign your own jurisdiction.
- Answer sheets—Each exercise includes an answer template at the end of the questions to make it easier to record and compile the answers.

The philosophy of the fifth edition remain the same as that of the prior editions. *Basic Legal Research Workbook* contains research exercises that allow students to learn about the scope and organization of research sources, guide them through the research process, and reinforce their skills through assignments requiring independent work.

The Workbook is designed to help students learn both the mechanics and the process of legal research through a combination of guided and unguided research assignments. In the guided assignments, the questions gradually increase in complexity. Review questions test students' understanding of the nature and organization of the sources they are using. Research questions early in an assignment direct students through the research process. Later questions ask for information, but require students to research more independently. The unguided research assignments require open research. Students generate their own search terms and follow their own research paths to locate legal authority.

Each assignment, whether guided or unguided, incorporates hypothetical fact patterns and legal questions that students must answer based on the results of their research. Thus, students must not only go through the steps of using each resource in an assignment, they must also read and apply what they find.

The Workbook's coverage is comprehensive. It contains exercises covering a wide range of legal research resources. Chapter 1 contains introductory assignments designed to acquaint students with the organization of the law library and basic features of cases and statutes. Chapter 2 contains information on generating search terms, as well as a series of charts that students can use to generate search terms for later assignments in this Workbook or any open research project.

Chapters 3 through 8 each contain three exercises. Chapter 3, Secondary Source Research, covers research with legal encyclopedias, A.L.R. Annotations, Restatements, legal periodicals, and treatises. Chapter 4, Case Research, addresses digest or subject and word searching. In Chapter 5, Research with Citators, students learn about citators for cases and other forms of authority. Chapter 6, Statutory Research, covers state and federal research. Chapter 7, Federal Legislative History Research, and Chapter 8, Federal Administrative Law Research, provide instruction in the most commonly used sources of federal law on these topics.

Chapter 9, Online Search Techniques, illustrates a variety of strategies for effective Boolean searching, including appropriate use of connectors and use of functions such as Field searches. It also demonstrates how to use Boolean searches in Westlaw, Lexis, and Bloomberg Law. Although it is the penultimate chapter, it can be assigned as soon as students have completed basic instruction in online research. Chapter 10 covers Research Planning. It contains hypothetical fact patterns that require students to develop and execute a research strategy using multiple sources of authority.

Each assignment follows a consistent organization that students should find easy to follow. In addition to containing research questions, each assignment also contains some textual material on the resource it covers. This is to provide context for the material and explain what students are likely to see in the books or online. The research questions in each assignment are fairly generic. Students use additional information in charts containing problem sets to answer the questions. Professors can assign problem sets or allow students to choose their own.

Additionally, the organization of each chapter gives professors the flexibility to assign exercises that fit with the structure and pace of their courses. Every exercise in every chapter is a free-standing assignment. Therefore, professors can assign the exercises in any order. The number of problem sets for each assignment adds to the Workbook's flexibility. Many exercises have multiple problem sets. For professors who coordinate instruction in research and writing, the problem sets cover a wide range of topics that can lend themselves to a number of potential writing projects.

Although *Basic Legal Research Workbook* contains some textual material interspersed with the research questions, it is not a self-instructional workbook. Students will need to read a research text, receive classroom instruction, or both to complete the assignments successfully and become adept at legal research. The Workbook is tailored to complement *Basic Legal Research: Tools and Strategies*. It can, however, be used with other research texts as well. In addition, the Workbook does not provide citation instruction. It covers research process, not citation format, although professors have the flexibility to require that citations conform to a designated citation format.

Both teaching and learning legal research are challenging undertakings. We hope that students using this Workbook will find it to be an engaging resource for learning the fundamentals of legal research. We hope professors will find it similarly engaging, as well as adaptable to a variety of course structures and teaching techniques.

Amy E. Sloan
Steven D. Schwinn
John D. Edwards
July 2016

Acknowledgments

Many people assisted us in writing the fifth edition of this text, and we would like to acknowledge their contributions. Our students, as always, inspire and guide us. We would also like to thank the people at Wolters Kluwer Legal Education who helped make this project a reality: Nicole Pinard, Donna Gridley, and their colleagues. We are indebted to The Froebe Group for both editorial and production support, with special thanks to Kathy Langone. The anonymous reviewers who took the time to share their experiences with prior editions of the text helped us tremendously, and we thank them as well.

Amy Sloan would like to thank a number of people who assisted with this book. The law librarians at the University of Baltimore School of Law were, as always, a great help. Special thanks go to Laura Cress for providing research assistance. She would also like to thank Peggy, Andrew, and Jack for the support and inspiration they provided.

Steven Schwinn would like to thank the faculty and staff at the John Marshall Law School Law Library. He would also like to thank Susie, Caroline, and Andrew for their support.

John Edwards would like to thank the faculty and staff of the Drake University Law Library. He would also like to express his appreciation to the Legal Research and Writing teaching assistants who tested assignments and made suggestions for improvement. Special thanks go to Kylie Crawford for her role in that process. Having the support of Beth Ann, Craig, Natasha, Martha, Chris, and Brooks helped make the project a success.

General Instructions

These general instructions explain the structure of the exercises in this Workbook and will help you get the most out of each assignment. You should read them before you start the first assignment and refer back to them as necessary for later assignments. Occasionally, the underlying research sources change so significantly that it is necessary to update the exercises. This is especially true for exercises covering online sources. Online sources are updated frequently, which means their look and coverage may change over time. You can check for updates at www.aspenlawschool.com/books/sloan_workbook.

I.   Using the Problem Set Charts

Many of the exercises contain multiple problem sets so that everyone in your class can work on the same assignment without needing to use the same materials at the same time. The research questions in the exercises are generic questions for all the problem sets. You will need to use additional information provided for your problem set to answer the questions.

The additional information for the problem sets appears in the problem set charts interspersed with the questions. Problem sets are identified by letter (A, B, C, etc.). If your professor does not assign a problem set for you to use, you can use any problem set to complete the assignment.

II.   Working on the Exercises

A.   Read the Learning Outcomes and Instructions

Each exercise begins with information about the assignment that you should read before you get started. The learning outcomes of the assignment and the specific instructions you should follow are set out at the beginning. The exercises will make the most sense to you if you know what you should get out of them and how to approach them. After the general instructions, you will find a section entitled "The Assignment." This section provides an overview of the assignment and should be reviewed before you begin your work.

B.   Answer the Questions

As you work on the questions, keep in mind that the answers should be fairly straightforward. If you find information that seems to answer a question, it probably answers the question. You should not expect the answers to jump off the page or screen, and you certainly need to read the questions carefully and follow all the research steps to answer them. The questions do not, however, contain hidden tricks or traps, and you should not read more into the questions than is there. The simplest answer will usually be the correct one.

Many of the questions contain hints to help you locate information to complete the exercise. The hints are intended to address aspects of the assignment that may raise questions. Be sure to read the hints carefully and follow them whenever they are provided.

Many of the questions require you to explain your answer. A simple yes or no will not suffice when the question asks for an explanation. Unless your professor requests something different, you should state your conclusion, summarize the legal rule on which you rely, and show how the facts of the hypothetical apply to the law. In most instances, you will be able to do this with a sentence or two of explanation.

For example, assume you were working on a research question asking whether a contract to sell illegal drugs is enforceable in court if it is breached, and assume you found a case saying that drug dealing contracts are not enforceable because they involve illegal activity. It would not be sufficient for you simply to answer "no" to the question. Instead, your answer should look something like this:

No. Courts will not enforce contracts to perform illegal activities. The drug dealing contract in this case involves illegal activity. Therefore, the courts will not enforce it.

C.   Ask for Help if You Get Sidetracked

Each exercise contains a time limit. Most of the time limits set the maximum amount of time you should spend working on individual questions. Some set the maximum amount of time you should spend on the entire exercise. **Follow these limits.** If you are taking longer than the time allotted to complete your work, you should stop and ask for help from your professor, a reference librarian, or another authorized person, such as a teaching assistant. Do not ask your classmates for help unless you are permitted to collaborate on research.

There are several common ways to get sidetracked on a research assignment. Following the troubleshooting hints below will help keep you from getting stuck in your research.

Some troubleshooting hints apply to all exercises, whether online or print:

- **Are you looking in the correct block in the problem set chart?** If not, you may be looking for something that does not exist in the jurisdiction or resource for your problem set.
- **Are you following any hints provided with the questions?** Be sure to read the hints carefully and follow them whenever they are provided.

When troubleshooting online research problems, these questions may be helpful:

- **Are you using the correct service and following the instructions for using that service?** If a question specifically directs you to use a particular research service, the instructions will not work for a different service.
- **Are you using the correct database, function, or command?** Although there is usually more than one way to locate an authority in an online source, the research questions are tailored to the databases, functions, and commands specified in the questions.

- **Have you typed the search information correctly?** Typographical and punctuation errors will affect the search results. If a research question directs you to use a specific search, be sure to enter it exactly as it appears in the exercise.

For print research, consider these troubleshooting questions:

- **Is the book you need off the shelf?** Someone else may be using the book, or it may be mis-shelved. A reference librarian can help you locate a missing book.
- **Are you looking in the correct book?** Be sure to check the volume number, if applicable. You should also check that you are using the correct edition or series in a set with multiple editions or series.
- **Are you looking in the correct place in the book?** Be sure to check the page number, if applicable. You should also check that you are looking in the right section if the book contains multiple types of information. If a research question directs you to use specific search terms in an index, be sure to use the search terms provided.
- **Have you remembered to follow every step in the research process for the resource you are using?** The most common reminder students need in conducting print research is, "Did you check the pocket part?"

Although following these hints will get you back on track in most situations, they may not always work. You should keep in mind that legal research is dynamic, but the exercises are static. Once they are printed, they cannot change to account for changes in the online interface, books, or applicable law. Therefore, if what you find does not seem to fit with the research questions, you should get help. You should also check online for any updates. If updates are available, you can find them at www.aspenlawschool.com/books/sloan_workbook.

Of course, starting an exercise well before it is due is another way to avoid difficulties. This is especially true for any exercises for which your professor instructs you to use print resources. Although most print exercises are structured to distribute students throughout the library, there are still likely to be at least some other students using the same resources you need to use. As the due date for an exercise approaches, books are more likely to be in use or mis-shelved, which will make completing the assignment more difficult. Most people, and especially lawyers, respond to deadline pressure and organize their work accordingly. If you can motivate yourself to do the work early, it will make these exercises easier for you.

Chapter 1
INTRODUCTION TO LEGAL RESEARCH

Exercise 1.1
Introduction to Print Research

Learning Outcomes

After completing this exercise, you should be able to

1. Distinguish among different types of authority.

2. Locate constitutional provisions, statutes, and cases in print from their citations.

3. Identify the formats of constitutional provisions, statutes, and cases.

Instructions

1. An answer sheet is provided at the end of the questions for your convenience while you are working on the exercise. After you finish your research, submit your answers in typewritten form on a separate answer sheet. Do not retype the questions. Your answer sheet should contain only the answers to the questions.

2. If you spend more than 15 minutes trying to find the answer to any individual question, use the troubleshooting hints in the General Instructions for this Workbook. If you are still unable to find the answer, stop and seek assistance.

3. Reshelve all books as soon as you finish using them.

Problem Sets

A B C D E F G H I J K L M N O

THE ASSIGNMENT

This exercise will acquaint you with the locations and formats of federal and state legal authorities. You will locate federal and state constitutions, statutes, and cases, and answer some questions about what you find.

I.   Review Questions

A.   Explain the difference between primary and secondary authorities, and give an example of each.

B.   Explain the difference between binding (or mandatory) and nonbinding (or persuasive) authorities, and give an example of each.

C.   When is secondary authority useful? Is it ever binding? Why or why not?

II.   Locating Federal Authorities in Print

A.   United States Constitution

The United States Constitution is the preeminent law of the land. All other laws, both federal and state, must comport with the federal Constitution. Because of its preeminence in the legal system, the federal Constitution is available in multiple sources and is often published along with statutes passed by legislatures in sets of books called "codes."

When Congress passes federal legislation, and the President signs it, the resulting statutes are published in the federal code, called the United States Code, which is discussed in more detail below. The federal Constitution is published with the federal code. State statutes are also published in codes. Every state has its own code. The federal Constitution is published in most (but not all) state codes.

For the questions below, you need to locate the federal Constitution in one of the code sets available in your library for your problem set. On this exercise you will use one of the unofficial versions—the *United States Code Annotated* (U.S.C.A.) or the *United States Code Service* (U.S.C.S.). Find the provision listed for your problem set in the following charts. When you locate the appropriate provisions in an unofficial version such as U.S.C.A. or U.S.C.S., you may see a series of notes following them, including summaries of cases interpreting the provisions. These notes are called "annotations." (That is why unofficial versions such as U.S.C.A. and U.S.C.S. are called "annotated codes.") You will learn to use these tools later in your legal research class. You do not need to read the annotations to answer the questions in this exercise.

You may also find a soft cover booklet called a "pocket part" inserted into the back cover of the annotated code. Pocket parts are used to update information in the hardcover volume. You will learn to use pocket parts later in your legal research class. You do not need to refer to the pocket part for this exercise.

Locate the provisions for your problem set in the United States Constitution to answer the questions below. If your library has neither the U.S.C.A. nor U.S.C.S., you may use an annotated state code that includes the United States Constitution.

United States Constitution

Problem Set A	Article I, § 1
Problem Set B	Article II, § 4
Problem Set C	Article III, § 1
Problem Set D	Article IV, § 1
Problem Set E	Amendment 1
Problem Set F	Amendment 2
Problem Set G	Amendment 4
Problem Set H	Amendment 5
Problem Set I	Amendment 6
Problem Set J	Amendment 7
Problem Set K	Amendment 10
Problem Set L	Amendment 13, § 1
Problem Set M	Amendment 14, § 2
Problem Set N	Amendment 16
Problem Set O	Amendment 19

1. Locate the listed provision in the United States Constitution. Briefly describe what this section provides.
2. Is this provision primary or secondary authority?
3. Is this provision binding or nonbinding authority for the state courts in the state where your law school is located?
4. Give the name of the code you used to find the answer and the copyright date of the volume.

B. Federal Statutes

As noted above, federal statutes are published in the federal code. You can find federal statutes using the *United States Code* (U.S.C.), the *United States Code Annotated* (U.S.C.A.), or the *United States Code Service* (U.S.C.S.).

When you locate a provision of the federal code, you may find annotations with research notes following the text of the provision. You will learn to use the annotations later in your legal research class. You do not need to read the annotations in order to answer the questions in this exercise.

You may also find a pocket part update inserted into the back cover of the book. You will learn to use pocket parts later in your research class. You do not need to refer to the pocket part for this exercise.

Locate the federal statute for your problem set, and answer the questions below. (Hint: If you use U.S.C. to answer the questions, be sure to use the most current edition.)

Federal Statutes—U.S.C., U.S.C.A., or U.S.C.S.

Problem Set A	Title 7, § 2029
Problem Set B	Title 8, § 1181
Problem Set C	Title 11, § 109
Problem Set D	Title 12, § 341
Problem Set E	Title 17, § 102
Problem Set F	Title 20, § 2005
Problem Set G	Title 21, § 361
Problem Set H	Title 26, § 61
Problem Set I	Title 28, § 1251
Problem Set J	Title 29, § 654
Problem Set K	Title 38, § 3481
Problem Set L	Title 42, § 2000a (Hint: Be sure to find § 2000a, not 2000(a) or 2000a-1, 2000a-2, etc.)
Problem Set M	Title 47, § 532
Problem Set N	Title 49, § 14502
Problem Set O	Title 50, § 2202

1. Provide the name of the section. You will find this next to the section number.
2. Briefly describe what the statute provides.
3. Give the name of the code you used to find the answer and the copyright date of the volume.

C.   Federal Cases

Federal cases are published in reporters. There are different sets of reporters for cases from different levels of the federal courts. (State cases are published in reporters, too. There are different sets of reporters for cases from different states. You will research state cases below, in IIIC.) For this exercise, you will need to locate one of the following sets of reporters: the *Federal Supplement* or *Federal Supplement*, 2d Series, both of which contain decisions from federal district courts, or the *Federal Reporter*, 2d Series, or *Federal Reporter*, 3d Series, both of which contain cases from the federal courts of appeals.

Locate the federal case for your problem set, and answer the questions below. (Hint: Be sure you are using both the correct reporter and the correct series to locate the federal case.)

Federal Cases

Problem Set A	*O'Connor v. Cindy Gerke & Associates, Inc.*, volume 300, *Federal Supplement*, 2d series, page 759
Problem Set B	*Midway Manufacturing Co. v. Strohon*, volume 564, *Federal Supplement*, page 741
Problem Set C	*Hunt v. Pasternack*, volume 179, *Federal Reporter*, 3d series, page 683
Problem Set D	*Torah Soft Ltd. v. Drosnin*, volume 136, *Federal Supplement*, 2d series, page 276
Problem Set E	*Tandy Corp. v. Personal Micro Computers, Inc.*, volume 524, *Federal Supplement*, page 171
Problem Set F	*Safeway, Inc. v. Occupational Safety & Health Review Comm'n*, volume 382, *Federal Reporter*, 3d series, page 1189
Problem Set G	*Anthony Crane Rental, Inc. v. Reich*, volume 70, *Federal Reporter*, 3d series, page 1298
Problem Set H	*Tierdael Construction Co. v. Occupational Safety and Health Review Comm'n*, volume 340, *Federal Reporter*, 3d series, page 1110
Problem Set I	*Brock v. Williams Enterprises of Georgia, Inc.*, volume 832, *Federal Reporter*, 2d series, page 567
Problem Set J	*Brock v. City Oil Well Service Co.*, volume 795, *Federal Reporter*, 2d series, page 507
Problem Set K	*Afkhami v. Carnival Corp.*, volume 305, *Federal Supplement*, 2d series, page 1308
Problem Set L	*Burnette v. Bredesen*, volume 566, *Federal Supplement*, 2d series, page 738
Problem Set M	*Sherman v. Marriott Hotel Services, Inc.*, volume 317, *Federal Supplement*, 2d series, page 609
Problem Set N	*Baker v. Greyhound Bus Line*, volume 240, *Federal Supplement*, 2d series, page 454
Problem Set O	*Rogers v. New York City Board of Elections*, volume 988, *Federal Supplement*, page 409

1. At the beginning of the case, you will see a synopsis of the decision. After the synopsis, you will see one or more paragraphs summarizing key points within the decision. A summary paragraph begins with a heading in bold type, followed by a key symbol and a number. If more than one summary paragraph appears at the beginning of the case, the paragraphs will be numbered. These summary paragraphs are research references called "headnotes" that you will learn to use later in your legal research class.

   How many headnotes are at the beginning of the case you located?

2. Following the headnote(s), you will find the name of the judge who wrote the opinion in the case. Provide the judge's name. (Hint: If the case has concurring or dissenting opinions, provide only the name of the judge who wrote the majority opinion.)

3. Briefly explain what this case is about. (Hint: Depending on which problem set you complete, the case may be quite long. Limit your explanation to 3-5 sentences. If the case has concurring or dissenting opinions, do not summarize them; limit your explanation to the majority opinion.)

III.   Locating State Authorities in Print

A.   State Constitutions

As noted above, all laws, both state and federal, must comport with the federal Constitution. Each state also has its own constitution. The constitution is created by a state constitutional convention, and it defines the authority granted to the state's government. All state laws must comport with that state's constitution. One place to find a state's constitution is in the state code.

When you locate a state constitutional provision, you may find annotations with research notes following the text of the provision. You will learn to use the annotations later in your legal research class. You do not need to read the annotations to answer the questions in this exercise.

You may also find a pocket part update inserted into the back cover of the book. You will learn to use pocket parts later in your legal research class. You do not need to refer to the pocket part for this exercise.

If your library has most state codes in print, your professor may assign you to use Chart A below. Chart B can be used if few print state codes outside your jurisdiction are available. Chart B assumes your law library will have the state code for the jurisdiction in which your school is located. Find your jurisdiction or one assigned by your instructor on the appropriate chart below. Use the state code and find the state constitution. Locate the provision indicated and answer the questions below. (Hint: Many state codes include old versions of the state constitution. Be sure to use the most recent version of the state constitution.)

State Constitutions

Chart A

Problem Set A	Arkansas	Article 2, § 6
Problem Set B	Indiana	Article 1, § 9
Problem Set C	Mississippi	Article 3, § 13
Problem Set D	New Mexico	Article II, § 17
Problem Set E	Michigan	Article I, § 5
Problem Set F	Connecticut	Article 1, § 4
Problem Set G	Georgia	Article I, § 1, Paragraph 5
Problem Set H	Florida	Article 1, § 4
Problem Set I	Colorado	Article 2, § 10

Problem Set J	Ohio	Article I, § 11
Problem Set K	Alabama	Article I, § 4
Problem Set L	North Carolina	Article I, § 14
Problem Set M	Iowa	Article 1, § 7
Problem Set N	Kentucky	§ 8
Problem Set O	Minnesota	Article 1, § 3

Chart B

Alabama	Article I, § 4	Montana	Article II, § 7
Alaska	Article I, § 5	Nebraska	Article I, § 5
Arizona	Article II, § 6	Nevada	Article 1, § 9
Arkansas	Article 2, § 6	New Hampshire	Article 22d
California	Article 1, § 2	New Jersey	Article I, § 6
Colorado	Article 2, § 10	New Mexico	Article II, § 17
Connecticut	Article 1, § 4	New York	Article I, § 8
Delaware	Article I, § 5	North Carolina	Article I, § 14
Florida	Article 1, § 4	North Dakota	Article I, § 4
Georgia	Article I, § 1, ¶ 5	Ohio	Article I, § 11
Hawaii	Article 1, § 4	Oklahoma	Article II, § 22
Idaho	Article 1, § 9	Oregon	Article I, § 8
Illinois	Article 1, § 4	Pennsylvania	Article I, § 7
Indiana	Article 1, § 9	Rhode Island	Article I, § 21
Iowa	Article 1, § 7	South Carolina	Article I, § 2
Kansas	Bill of Rights § 11	South Dakota	Article VI, § 5
Kentucky	§ 8	Tennessee	Article I, § 19
Louisiana	Article 1, § 7	Texas	Article I, § 8
Maine	Article 1, § 4	Utah	Article I, § 15
Maryland	Declaration of Rights Article 40	Vermont	Chapter I, Article 13
Massachusetts	Article XVI (Hint: Use the Part of the First, not the Articles of Amendment.)	Virginia	Article I, § 12

Michigan	Article I, § 5	Washington	Article I, § 5
Minnesota	Article 1, § 3	West Virginia	Article III, § 7
Mississippi	Article 3, § 13	Wisconsin	Article I, § 3
Missouri	Article I, § 8	Wyoming	Article I, § 20

1. Briefly describe what the provision says.
2. Is this provision of the state constitution primary or secondary authority?
3. Is this provision of the state constitution binding or nonbinding authority for the state courts in that state?
4. Give the name of the code you used to find the answer and the copyright date of the volume.

B.   State Statutes

As noted above, when a state legislature passes legislation (pursuant to power granted to it by the state constitution), the resulting statutes are published in the state code.

When you locate a provision of a state code, you may find annotations with research notes following the text of the provision. You will learn to use annotations later in your legal research class. You do not need to read the annotations to answer the questions in this exercise.

You may also find a pocket part update inserted into the back cover of the book. You will learn to use pocket parts later in your legal research class. You do not need to refer to the pocket part for this exercise.

If your library has most state codes in print, your professor may assign you to use Chart A below. Your library may have a different version of the state code that can be used to answer the question. Chart B can be used if few print state codes outside your jurisdiction are available. Chart B assumes your law library will have the state code for the jurisdiction in which your school is located. Find your jurisdiction or one assigned by your instructor on the appropriate chart below. Locate the state statute for your problem set or assigned jurisdiction, and answer the questions below.

State Codes

Chart A

Problem Set A	*Arkansas Code of 1987 Annotated § 5-39-201*
Problem Set B	*Burns Indiana Statutes Annotated § 35-43-2-1*
Problem Set C	*Mississippi Code 1972 Annotated or West's Annotated Mississippi Code § 97-17-23*
Problem Set D	*New Mexico Statutes 1978 Annotated § 30-16-3*
Problem Set E	*Michigan Compiled Laws Annotated § 750.110*
Problem Set F	*Connecticut General Statutes Annotated § 42a-2-302*

Problem Set G	*Official Code of Georgia Annotated § 11-2-302*
Problem Set H	*West's Florida Statutes Annotated § 672.302*
Problem Set I	*Colorado Revised Statutes Annotated § 4-2-302*
Problem Set J	*Baldwin's or Page's Ohio Revised Code Annotated § 1302.15*
Problem Set K	*Code of Alabama of 1975 § 6-11-20*
Problem Set L	*General Statutes of North Carolina Annotated § 1D-15*
Problem Set M	*Iowa Code Annotated § 668A.1*
Problem Set N	*Baldwin's or Michie's Kentucky Revised Statutes Annotated § 411.186*
Problem Set O	*Minnesota Statutes Annotated § 549.20*

Chart B

Alabama	§ 13A-8-41	Montana	§ 45-5-401
Alaska	§ 11.41.500	Nebraska	§ 28-324
Arizona	§ 13-1902	Nevada	§ 200.380
Arkansas	§ 5-12-102	New Hampshire	§ 636:1
California	Penal § 212.5	New Jersey	§ 2C:15-1
Colorado	§ 18-4-301	New Mexico	§ 30-16-2
Connecticut	§ 53a-133	New York	Penal § 160.00
Delaware	tit. 11, § 831	North Carolina	§ 14-87
Florida	§ 812.13	North Dakota	§ 12.1-22-01
Georgia	§ 16-8-40	Ohio	§ 2911.01
Hawaii	§ 708-840	Oklahoma	tit. 21, § 791
Idaho	§ 18-6501	Oregon	§ 164.415
Illinois	ch. 720, § 5/18-1	Pennsylvania	tit. 18, § 3701
Indiana	§ 35-42-5-1	Rhode Island	§ 11-39-1
Iowa	§ 711.1	South Carolina	§ 16-11-325
Kansas	§ 21-5420	South Dakota	§ 22-30-1
Kentucky	§ 15.050	Tennessee	§ 39-13-401
Louisiana	§ 14:64	Texas	Penal § 29.02
Maine	tit. 17-A, § 651	Utah	§ 76-6-301
Maryland	Crim. Law § 3-402	Vermont	tit. 13, § 608

Massachusetts	ch. 265, § 17	Virginia	§ 18.2.58 (Hint: Locate § 18.2.58, not 18.2.58.1.)
Michigan	§ 750.529	Washington	§ 9A.56.200
Minnesota	§ 609.24	West Virginia	§ 61-2-12
Mississippi	§ 97-3-73	Wisconsin	§ 943.32
Missouri	§ 569.020	Wyoming	§ 6-2-401

1. Provide the name of the section. You will find this next to the section number.
2. Briefly describe what this section provides.
3. Give the name of the code you used to find the answer and the copyright date of the volume.

C.   State Cases

As noted above, state court opinions, like federal court opinions, are published in books called "reporters." Some states publish reporters containing only cases decided by the courts of that state. There are also sets of reporters called "regional reporters" that compile cases from several states within a particular geographic region. To answer the following questions, you will need to find the regional reporters.

Locate the state case for your problem set, and answer the questions below. (Hint: The regional reporters have multiple series (2d, 3d). When you locate the reporter, be sure you are looking in the correct series.)

State Case

Problem Set A	*Winters v. State*, volume 848, *South Western Reporter*, 2d series, page 441
Problem Set B	*Gebhart v. State*, volume 525, *North Eastern Reporter*, 2d series, page 603
Problem Set C	*Wheeler v. State*, volume 826, *Southern Reporter*, 2d series, page 731
Problem Set D	*State v. Gregory*, volume 869, *Pacific Reporter*, 2d series, page 292
Problem Set E	*People v. Toole*, volume 576, *North Western Reporter*, 2d series, page 441
Problem Set F	*Iamartino v. Avallone*, volume 477, *Atlantic Reporter*, 2d series, page 124
Problem Set G	*Stefan Jewelers, Inc. v. Electro-Protective Corp.*, volume 288, *South Eastern Reporter*, 2d series, page 667
Problem Set H	*Credit Alliance Corp. v. Westland Mach. Co., Inc.*, volume 439, *Southern Reporter*, 2d series, page 332
Problem Set I	*Davis v. M.L.G. Corp.*, volume 712, *Pacific Reporter*, 2d series, page 985

Problem Set J	*Spectrum Networks, Inc. v. Plus Realty, Cincinnati, Inc.*, volume 878, *North Eastern Reporter*, 2d series, page 1122
Problem Set K	*Clark v. Kindley*, volume 10, *Southern Reporter*, 3d series, page 1005
Problem Set L	*Phillips v. Restaurant Management of Carolina, L.P.*, volume 552, *South Eastern Reporter*, 2d series, page 686
Problem Set M	*Kuta v. Newberg*, volume 600, *North Western Reporter*, 2d series, page 280
Problem Set N	*Bierman v. Klapheke*, volume 967, *South Western Reporter*, 2d series, page 16
Problem Set O	*Wikert v. Northern Sand and Gravel, Inc.*, volume 402, *North Western Reporter*, 2d series, page 178

1. Following the name of the case, you will find a reference to the name of the court that decided this case. Provide the name of the court.

2. You will find one or more headnotes at the beginning of the case. How many headnotes are at the beginning of the case you located?

3. Briefly explain what this case is about. If you used one of the problem sets in Chart A, explain how the case relates to the state statute you located. If you used one of the jurisdictions in Chart B, briefly summarize the case. (Hint: Depending on which problem set you complete, the case may be quite long. Limit your explanation to 3-5 sentences. If the case has concurring or dissenting opinions, do not summarize them; limit your explanation to the majority opinion.)

Exercise 1.1
Introduction to Print Research

Name: _____   Due Date: _____

Professor: _____   Section: _____

Problem Set: _____

I.   Review Questions

A.

B.

C.

II.   Locating Federal Authorities in Print

A.   United States Constitution

A.1.

A.2.

A.3.

A.4.

B.   Federal Statutes

B.1.

B.2.

B.3.

C.   Federal Cases

C.1.

C.2.

C.3.

III.   Locating State Authorities in Print

A.   State Constitutions

A.1.

A.2.

A.3.

A.4.

B.   State Statutes

B.1.

B.2.

B.3.

C.   State Cases

C.1.

C.2.

C.3.

Exercise 1.2
Introduction to Online Research

Learning Outcomes

After completing this exercise, you should be able to

1. Retrieve authorities in Westlaw, Lexis, and Bloomberg Law from their citations.

2. Identify the formats of authorities in Westlaw, Lexis, and Bloomberg Law.

3. Use some of the navigation tools in Westlaw, Lexis, and Bloomberg Law to link both to information within the retrieved document and to new documents referenced within the retrieved document.

Instructions

1. An answer sheet is provided at the end of the questions for your convenience while you are working on the exercise. After you finish your research, submit your answers in typewritten form on a separate answer sheet. Do not retype the questions. Your answer sheet should contain only the answers to the questions.

2. If you spend more than 15 minutes trying to find the answer to any individual question, use the troubleshooting hints in the General Instructions for this Workbook. If you are still unable to find the answer, stop and seek assistance.

Problem Sets

A B C D E F G H I J K L M N O

THE ASSIGNMENT

This exercise requires you to retrieve legal authorities using three of the most commonly used online research services, Westlaw, Lexis, and Bloomberg Law. Although the text of an authority retrieved using any one of these services will be identical, each service adds its own editorial enhancements and research links to help you locate additional information related to the authority. As a consequence, the format of a document retrieved using one of these services may differ slightly from the format of the same document retrieved in the other.

I. Westlaw

A. Locating Cases in Westlaw

Use the global search box in Westlaw to retrieve a state case from its citation. Retrieve any state case for your problem set. If you completed Exercise 1.1, choose any case for your problem set **other than** the one you located in print in Exercise 1.1. Do not enter the case name; use only the abbreviated citation provided in the problem set to retrieve the case.

State Case

Problem Sets A, B, C, D & E	(1) *Winters v. State*, 848 S.W.2d 441
	(2) *Gebhart v. State*, 525 N.E.2d 603
	(3) *Wheeler v. State*, 826 So. 2d 731
	(4) *State v. Gregory*, 869 P.2d 292
	(5) *People v. Toole*, 576 N.W.2d 441
Problem Sets F, G, H, I & J	(1) *Iamartino v. Avallone*, 477 A.2d 124
	(2) *Stefan Jewelers, Inc. v. Electro-Protective Corp.*, 288 S.E.2d 667
	(3) *Credit Alliance Corp. v. Westland Mach. Co., Inc.*, 439 So. 2d 332
	(4) *Davis v. M.L.G. Corp.*, 712 P.2d 985
	(5) *Spectrum Networks, Inc. v. Plus Realty, Cincinnati, Inc.*, 878 N.E.2d 1122
Problem Sets K, L, M, N & O	(1) *Clark v. Kindley*, 10 So. 3d 1005
	(2) *Phillips v. Restaurant Management of Carolina, L.P.*, 552 S.E.2d 686
	(3) *Kuta v. Newberg*, 600 N.W.2d 280
	(4) *Bierman v. Klapheke*, 967 S.W.2d 16
	(5) *Wikert v. Northern Sand and Gravel, Inc.*, 402 N.W.2d 178

1. Provide the name of the court that decided the case.

2. At the beginning of the case, you will see a synopsis of the decision. After the synopsis, you will see one or more paragraphs summarizing key points within the decision. A summary paragraph begins with a subject heading in bold type, followed by a key symbol and a number or subject subheading. The paragraphs will be numbered. These summary paragraphs are research references called "headnotes" that you will learn to use later in your legal research class.

   How many headnotes appear at the beginning of the case?

3. Read the first headnote in the case. You can use the headnotes to navigate within the case. Click on the 1 in the box with the first headnote in the case.

   Where does this link take you within the document?

B.   Locating Statutes in Westlaw

Use the global search box in Westlaw to retrieve a state statute from its citation.

Retrieve any state statute for your problem set. If you completed Exercise 1.1, choose any statute for your problem set **other than** one you located in Exercise 1.1. Use the abbreviated citation provided in the problem set to retrieve the statute.

State Statute

Problem Sets A, B, C, D & E	(1) AR ST 5-39-201 (2) IN ST 35-43-2-1 (3) MS ST 97-17-23 (4) NM ST 30-16-3 (5) MI ST 750.110	(Hint: Locate section 35-43-2-1, not 35-43-2-1.5.)
Problem Sets F, G, H, I & J	(1) CT ST 42a-2-302 (2) GA ST 11-2-302 (3) FL ST 672.302 (4) CO ST 4-2-302 (5) OH ST 1302.15	
Problem Sets K, L, M, N & O	(1) AL ST 6-11-20 (2) NC ST 1D-15 (3) IA ST 668A.1 (4) KY ST 411.186 (5) MN ST 549.20	

1. Briefly describe what the statute provides.

2. Sometimes you will find research notes called annotations following the text of the statute, including summaries of cases that have interpreted the statute. Locate case summaries in the annotations following the statute you retrieved by clicking on the "Notes of Decisions" tab.

   Click on the link to any case in the annotations. Provide the name of the case you selected, and briefly describe the case.

II.   Lexis

A.   Locating Cases in Lexis

Retrieve the same case you retrieved in Westlaw for Question IA, above. Again, enter only the abbreviated citation to retrieve the case. The citations are repeated below.

To locate a case by citation, enter the abbreviated citation in the Lexis red search box and execute the search. Note that Lexis may display the state reporter citation instead of the regional reporter citation next to the case name.

State Case

Problem Sets A, B, C, D & E	(1) *Winters v. State*, 848 S.W.2d 441
	(2) *Gebhart v. State*, 525 N.E.2d 603
	(3) *Wheeler v. State*, 826 So. 2d 731
	(4) *State v. Gregory*, 869 P.2d 292
	(5) *People v. Toole*, 576 N.W.2d 441
Problem Sets F, G, H, I & J	(1) *Iamartino v. Avallone*, 477 A.2d 124
	(2) *Stefan Jewelers, Inc. v. Electro-Protective Corp.*, 288 S.E.2d 667
	(3) *Credit Alliance Corp. v. Westland Mach. Co., Inc.*, 439 So. 2d 332
	(4) *Davis v. M.L.G. Corp.*, 712 P.2d 985
	(5) *Spectrum Networks, Inc. v. Plus Realty, Cincinnati, Inc.*, 878 N.E.2d 1122
Problem Sets K, L, M, N & O	(1) *Clark v. Kindley*, 10 So. 3d 1005
	(2) *Phillips v. Restaurant Management of Carolina, L.P.*, 552 S.E.2d 686
	(3) *Kuta v. Newberg*, 600 N.W.2d 280
	(4) *Bierman v. Klapheke*, 967 S.W.2d 16
	(5) *Wikert v. Northern Sand and Gravel, Inc.*, 402 N.W.2d 178

1. Briefly describe what the case is about.

2. List at least two format differences you notice between the Lexis and Westlaw versions of this case.

3. After the sections summarizing the decision, you will see a list of LexisNexis Headnotes similar to West headnotes. Read the first headnote and then click on the blue downward arrow next to it. Where does this link take you within the document?

B.   Locating Statutes in Lexis

Use Lexis to retrieve a federal statute from its citation. To do this, enter the abbreviated citation for your problem set in the chart below in the red search box and execute the search.

Federal Statute

Problem Sets A, B, C, D & E	17 uscs 102 (Retrieve the statutory provision, not the "Revised Title Table.")
Problem Sets F, G, H, I & J	29 uscs 654
Problem Sets K, L, M, N & O	42 uscs 2000a (Hint: Be sure to find § 2000a, not 2000(a) or 2000a-1, 2000a-2, etc.)

1. Briefly describe what the statute provides.

2. Sometimes you will find research notes called annotations following the text of the statute, including summaries of cases that have interpreted the statute. Locate case summaries in the annotations following the statute you retrieved. Case summaries appear after the section in the annotations called "Case Notes." You can find this section by scrolling through the document or by using the option to "Go to" the Case Notes. Click on the blue downward arrow next to any topic in the Case Notes, or scroll past the list of Case Notes topics to the case summaries.

   Click on the link to any case in the annotations. Provide the name of the case you selected, and briefly describe the case.

III.   Bloomberg Law

A.   Locating Cases in Bloomberg Law

Retrieve the same case you retrieved in Lexis for Question IIA, above. To do this, enter the abbreviated citation for your problem set in the chart below in the Bloomberg <GO> bar and execute the search.

State Case

Problem Sets A, B, C, D & E	(1) *Winters v. State*, 848 S.W.2d 441 (2) *Gebhart v. State*, 525 N.E.2d 603 (3) *Wheeler v. State*, 826 So. 2d 731 (4) *State v. Gregory*, 869 P.2d 292 (5) *People v. Toole*, 576 N.W.2d 441
Problem Sets F, G, H, I & J	(1) *Iamartino v. Avallone*, 477 A.2d 124 (2) *Stefan Jewelers, Inc. v. Electro-Protective Corp.*, 288 S.E.2d 667 (3) *Credit Alliance Corp. v. Westland Mach. Co., Inc.*, 439 So. 2d 332 (4) *Davis v. M.L.G. Corp.*, 712 P.2d 985 (5) *Spectrum Networks, Inc. v. Plus Realty, Cincinnati, Inc.*, 878 N.E.2d 1122
Problem Sets K, L, M, N & O	(1) *Clark v. Kindley*, 10 So. 3d 1005 (2) *Phillips v. Restaurant Management of Carolina, L.P.*, 552 S.E.2d 686 (3) *Kuta v. Newberg*, 600 N.W.2d 280 (4) *Bierman v. Klapheke*, 967 S.W.2d 16 (5) *Wikert v. Northern Sand and Gravel, Inc.*, 402 N.W.2d 178

1. What is the name of the judge who wrote the opinion? (Hint: Some opinions are unsigned. If the opinion you located is unsigned, answer "Per Curiam.")

2. What year was the case decided?

3. Highlight the last few lines of the text of the opinion. What words appear in a box on top of the text? What happens when you click on that box?

B.   Locating Statutes in Bloomberg Law

Use Bloomberg Law to retrieve a federal statute from its citation. To do this, enter the abbreviated citation for your problem set in the chart below in the <GO> bar and execute the search. Review the search results to locate the correct section.

Federal Statute

Problem Sets A, B, C, D & E	17 usc 102
Problem Sets F, G, H, I & J	29 usc 654
Problem Sets K, L, M, N & O	42 usc 2000a (Hint: Be sure to find § 2000a, not 2000(a) or 2000a-1, 2000a-2, etc.)

1. List at least one similarity and one difference you notice between the Lexis and Bloomberg Law versions of the statute.

2. What information do you get when you click on the "Smart Code" tab?

Exercise 1.2
Introduction to Online Research

Name: _____   Due Date: _____

Professor: _____   Section: _____

Problem Set: _____

I. Westlaw

A.   Locating Cases in Westlaw

A.1.

A.2.

A.3.

B.   Locating Statutes in Westlaw

B.1.

B.2.

II.   Lexis

A.   Locating Cases in Lexis

A.1.

A.2.

A.3.

B.   Locating Statutes in Lexis

B.1.

B.2.

III.   Bloomberg Law

A.   Locating Cases in Bloomberg Law

A.1.

A.2.

A.3.

B.   Locating Statutes in Bloomberg Law

B.1.

B.2.

Chapter 2
GENERATING SEARCH TERMS

Exercise 2.1
Generating Search Terms

Learning Outcome

After completing this exercise, you should be able to generate search terms from a set of facts surrounding a legal question.

Instructions

The charts included in this exercise contain space for you to write. This is for your convenience while you are working on the exercise. After you finish the exercise, you must submit your answers in typewritten form on a separate answer sheet. Do not retype the chart. Submit your answers in the format specified by your professor.

There are no separate problem sets for this exercise.

THE ASSIGNMENT

In legal research, one of the first steps in the research process is generating a list of search terms. You need to use search terms to locate information in a subject index, table of contents, or online database. This exercise contains charts you can use to generate search terms.

Legal information is often organized by category, so one technique that can help you generate useful search terms is organizing the facts of a legal problem by category. Once you have organized your information by category, you can expand the list to include additional terms. You can expand the list by increasing the breadth and depth of the search terms. You can increase the breadth by brainstorming synonyms or related concepts. You can increase the depth by expressing ideas with varying degrees of abstraction. Here are two examples:

Initial search term	hotel
Terms generated by increasing breadth with synonyms or related terms	motel inn

Initial search term	theft
Terms generated by varying the level of abstraction	robbery (less abstract) crime (more abstract)

The charts that follow list categories of information that can help you generate search terms for effective research. You can use the charts for any of the exercises in this Workbook that require you to generate search terms. You can also use them for other research projects. Several copies of the chart are provided on the following pages.

Chart 1

Categories of information	Initial search terms	Increased breadth (synonyms or related terms)	Increased depth (varying degrees of abstraction)
Parties involved • Describe parties according to their relationships to each other (e.g., landlord and tenant)			
Places and things These can include the following: • Geographic location (e.g., Pennsylvania) • Type of location (e.g., school or church) • Tangible objects (e.g., automobiles) • Intangible concepts (e.g., vacation or reputation)			
Potential claims and defenses If these are not apparent, consider the following: • Parties' conduct (acts done and not done) • Parties' mental states • Injury suffered			
Relief sought by the complaining or injured party			
Additional categories:			

Chart 2

Categories of information	Initial search terms	Increased breadth (synonyms or related terms)	Increased depth (varying degrees of abstraction)
Parties involved • Describe parties according to their relationships to each other (e.g., landlord and tenant)			
Places and things These can include the following: • Geographic location (e.g., Pennsylvania) • Type of location (e.g., school or church) • Tangible objects (e.g., automobiles) • Intangible concepts (e.g., vacation or reputation)			
Potential claims and defenses If these are not apparent, consider the following: • Parties' conduct (acts done and not done) • Parties' mental states • Injury suffered			
Relief sought by the complaining or injured party			
Additional categories:			

Chart 3

Categories of information	Initial search terms	Increased breadth (synonyms or related terms)	Increased depth (varying degrees of abstraction)
Parties involved • Describe parties according to their relationships to each other (e.g., landlord and tenant)			
Places and things These can include the following: • Geographic location (e.g., Pennsylvania) • Type of location (e.g., school or church) • Tangible objects (e.g., automobiles) • Intangible concepts (e.g., vacation or reputation)			
Potential claims and defenses If these are not apparent, consider the following: • Parties' conduct (acts done and not done) • Parties' mental states • Injury suffered			
Relief sought by the complaining or injured party			
Additional categories:			

Chart 4

Categories of information	Initial search terms	Increased breadth (synonyms or related terms)	Increased depth (varying degrees of abstraction)
Parties involved • Describe parties according to their relationships to each other (e.g., landlord and tenant)			
Places and things These can include the following: • Geographic location (e.g., Pennsylvania) • Type of location (e.g., school or church) • Tangible objects (e.g., automobiles) • Intangible concepts (e.g., vacation or reputation)			
Potential claims and defenses If these are not apparent, consider the following: • Parties' conduct (acts done and not done) • Parties' mental states • Injury suffered			
Relief sought by the complaining or injured party			
Additional categories:			

Chart 5

Categories of information	Initial search terms	Increased breadth (synonyms or related terms)	Increased depth (varying degrees of abstraction)
Parties involved • Describe parties according to their relationships to each other (e.g., landlord and tenant)			
Places and things These can include the following: • Geographic location (e.g., Pennsylvania) • Type of location (e.g., school or church) • Tangible objects (e.g., automobiles) • Intangible concepts (e.g., vacation or reputation)			
Potential claims and defenses If these are not apparent, consider the following: • Parties' conduct (acts done and not done) • Parties' mental states • Injury suffered			
Relief sought by the complaining or injured party			
Additional categories:			

Chart 6

Categories of information	Initial search terms	Increased breadth (synonyms or related terms)	Increased depth (varying degrees of abstraction)
Parties involved • Describe parties according to their relationships to each other (e.g., landlord and tenant)			
Places and things These can include the following: • Geographic location (e.g., Pennsylvania) • Type of location (e.g., school or church) • Tangible objects (e.g., automobiles) • Intangible concepts (e.g., vacation or reputation)			
Potential claims and defenses If these are not apparent, consider the following: • Parties' conduct (acts done and not done) • Parties' mental states • Injury suffered			
Relief sought by the complaining or injured party			
Additional categories:			

Chart 7

Categories of information	Initial search terms	Increased breadth (synonyms or related terms)	Increased depth (varying degrees of abstraction)
Parties involved • Describe parties according to their relationships to each other (e.g., landlord and tenant)			
Places and things These can include the following: • Geographic location (e.g., Pennsylvania) • Type of location (e.g., school or church) • Tangible objects (e.g., automobiles) • Intangible concepts (e.g., vacation or reputation)			
Potential claims and defenses If these are not apparent, consider the following: • Parties' conduct (acts done and not done) • Parties' mental states • Injury suffered			
Relief sought by the complaining or injured party			
Additional categories:			

Chart 8

Categories of information	Initial search terms	Increased breadth (synonyms or related terms)	Increased depth (varying degrees of abstraction)
Parties involved • Describe parties according to their relationships to each other (e.g., landlord and tenant)			
Places and things These can include the following: • Geographic location (e.g., Pennsylvania) • Type of location (e.g., school or church) • Tangible objects (e.g., automobiles) • Intangible concepts (e.g., vacation or reputation)			
Potential claims and defenses If these are not apparent, consider the following: • Parties' conduct (acts done and not done) • Parties' mental states • Injury suffered			
Relief sought by the complaining or injured party			
Additional categories:			

Chapter 3
SECONDARY SOURCE RESEARCH

Exercise 3.1
Researching Secondary Sources Online
with Table of Contents and Word Searches

Learning Outcomes

After completing this exercise, you should be able to

1. Use Westlaw, Lexis, and subscription databases to locate secondary sources using table of contents and word searches.

2. Navigate through a secondary source retrieved online to locate information within the source.

Instructions

1. An answer sheet is provided at the end of the questions for your convenience while you are working on the exercise. After you finish your research, submit your answers in typewritten form on a separate answer sheet. Do not retype the questions. Your answer sheet should contain only the answers to the questions.

2. If you spend more than 15 minutes trying to find the answer to any individual question, use the troubleshooting hints in the General Instructions for this Workbook. If you are still unable to find the answer, stop and seek assistance.

There are no separate problem sets for this exercise.

For this exercise, you will conduct research on secondary sources online. Online research tools can be very useful in locating secondary sources. Am. Jur. 2d, C.J.S., A.L.R. Annotations, Restatements of the law, many legal periodicals, and many treatises are available online. Although online tools can be useful for researching secondary sources, they also have some limitations. For example, not all secondary sources are available online.

This exercise introduces you to online search techniques for secondary sources. There are three common search techniques for researching secondary sources online: (1) browsing a document's table of contents; (2) executing a word search; and (3) retrieving a document from its citation. This exercise illustrates table of contents and word searching. Exercise 3.2, below, covers retrieving authorities from their citations.

THE ASSIGNMENT

A client has come to you with the matter below, and you need to research this issue.

Georgia Stevens, a 23-year-old grad student, recently visited the emergency room at Granville Hospital, a for-profit hospital, for treatment of a migraine headache. Dr. Paula Villar was Stevens' attending physician, and Nurse Kevin Johnson was her principal nurse.

Upon instructions from Dr. Villar, Nurse Johnson administered two drugs to Stevens, one for pain, and one for nausea. Dr. Villar ordered Nurse Johnson to administer the drugs by injecting them directly into Stevens' arm. This method of delivery is called "IV push."

The nausea drug, however, comes with a manufacturer's statement that warns against administering the drug by IV push. The statement says that IV push creates an intolerably high risk of irreversible gangrene if the drug comes into contact with arterial blood. The statement says that the drug should only be administered through an IV drip.

In attempting to inject the drugs into Stevens' vein, consistent with Dr. Villar's orders, Nurse Johnson accidentally struck an artery. Stevens developed gangrene in her forearm and hand as a result of Nurse Johnson's intra-arterial injection of these drugs. Doctors had to amputate Stevens' arm below the elbow.

Stevens asks you whether she can bring a claim against Granville hospital for Dr. Villar's and Nurse Johnson's negligence in administering these drugs. You learned that Dr. Villar is an independent contractor (and not an employee) of the hospital, but that Nurse Johnson is a full-time employee. You need to research the doctrine of vicarious liability, and, in particular, respondeat superior.

Because vicarious liability is a doctrine with which you may not be familiar, researching secondary sources would be a good way to begin. The secondary sources you research for this exercise will not provide enough information to answer your client's question. You would need to research primary authority to answer the question. This exercise simply illustrates how secondary sources can be used to obtain background information on a subject and to locate references to primary authority.

I.   Review Questions

A.   Briefly explain why secondary sources are often a good starting point for your legal research on a problem.

B.   Briefly explain the key differences between legal encyclopedias, A.L.R. Annotations, and legal periodicals.

C.   What is a Restatement of the Law? Why might you use a Restatement in your legal research?

II.   Westlaw

A.   Searching a Legal Encyclopedia Using the Table of Contents

One resource that can be a useful starting point for a research project is a legal encyclopedia. Legal encyclopedias simply report on the state of the law in a very general way. They are helpful for obtaining general background information on your research topic and for locating limited citations to primary legal authority.

To obtain an overview of the doctrines of vicarious liability and respondeat superior, you might begin your research with a legal encyclopedia. Both the Am. Jur. 2d and C.J.S. legal encyclopedias are available online in Westlaw. Am. Jur. 2d is also available online in Lexis. One way to research using a legal encyclopedia is to browse the publication's table of contents.

In Westlaw, from the "All Content" tab, follow the links to "Secondary Sources," "Texts & Treatises," and "American Jurisprudence 2d." This will bring up the table of contents.

From the main table of contents, one subject that might help with your research into the client matter is "Employment Relationship." From the "Employment Relationship" entry, drill down through each of the following choices to retrieve a section from Am. Jur. 2d:

> Liability of Employer to Third Party
>
> Vicarious Liability
>
> In General
>
> Liability of employer under respondeat superior

1. Review the section of Am. Jur. 2d that you retrieved. Provide the section number.
2. What does the respondeat superior doctrine state generally?
3. According to the section you retrieved, the principles of respondeat superior apply when the claim is based in tort or negligence and the plaintiff alleges that the employer is liable for the conduct of an employee because the employee was acting within the scope of employment. Provide the name and citation of a case from Kentucky that supports this proposition.

     (Hint: In Westlaw, place the cursor over the footnote number to display the footnote information supporting the textual statement. Use the reporter abbreviations to identify a case decided by a Kentucky (Ky.) court.)
4. Use the link near the top of the screen to advance to the next section of Am. Jur. 2d. (Hint: Look for the green triangles next to the §.)

     According to this section, what are the four general factors that bear upon whether a master-servant relationship exists for purposes of the doctrine of respondeat superior?

B.   Locating A.L.R. Annotations Using Word Searches

American Law Reports, or A.L.R., Annotations collect summaries of cases, typically from a variety of jurisdictions, to provide an overview of the law on a narrow topic. Unlike legal encyclopedias, which usually focus on very broad topics, A.L.R. Annotations tend to focus on narrower legal questions. A.L.R. Annotations are also more detailed than legal encyclopedia entries because they include summaries of specific cases. Like encyclopedia entries, however, they do not contain much analysis. They simply report the results of decisions. A.L.R. Annotations can be a helpful way to begin your legal research to give you an overview of your research topic as well as providing authorities on both sides of an issue. They can also direct you to primary authority from the controlling jurisdiction and persuasive authority from other jurisdictions.

Although most A.L.R. Annotations are also available in Lexis, the first series is not, so Westlaw should be used on this exercise.

You decide to continue your research on respondeat superior in the A.L.R. Annotations in Westlaw. You are especially interested in learning more details about how the doctrine applies in medical malpractice cases, and whether Granville could be vicariously liable for Dr. Villar's negligence. A.L.R. Annotations are a good place to look for this kind of information.

To answer the questions below, you need to locate the A.L.R. database.

In Westlaw from the "All Content" tab, follow the links for "Secondary Sources" and "American Law Reports."

Execute the following search:

> When can a hospital be vicariously liable for the negligence of a physician?

1. Review the first 10 items in the search results. Provide the title and citation of the Annotation that seems most relevant to the question when a hospital can be liable for the negligence of a physician.

2. Click on the link to open this Annotation. Provide the name of the author of the Annotation.

3. To locate information in an Annotation, you can scroll through the document or use the links to the navigation tools listed in the "Table of Contents" section near the beginning of the document. For this question, use the Article Outline to locate the link to the heading for "Where physician is independent contractor." Click on the section for "Rule of nonliability, generally." What do the cases in this section hold or recognize?

4. Now return to the Article Outline and the section discussing "Where physician is independent contractor." What is covered by the other two sections and why might you want to review them?

C.   Researching Multiple Secondary Sources

Using Westlaw, you can research a variety of secondary sources, including encyclopedias, A.L.R. Annotations, and treatises with a single search. The search results can be limited by jurisdiction, but the search will retrieve many types of authority (statutes, cases, secondary sources, etc.). The advantage to this approach is that it allows you to retrieve multiple forms of authority in a single search. When you are not sure what type of authority will help you answer a research question or when you know you need multiple types of authority, a global search can be effective. The disadvantage is that having all results in a single search may make it difficult to focus on the most relevant or most authoritative sources.

You must evaluate the results carefully to make sure you locate and use the best authority available to resolve your research issue.

To continue your research into secondary sources that discuss vicarious liability and respondeat superior, enter the following search in the Westlaw search box:

vicarious liability and medical malpractice

(Hint: If you have just completed Section A or B of this part of the exercise, be sure to reset your content. You can do this by clicking the content box to the left of the search box and selecting "All Content." Also be sure to reset your jurisdictions. You can do this by clicking the jurisdiction box to the right of the search box and selecting "All States" and "All Federal.")

1. Using the filtering options under "View," display the "Secondary Sources" results. Using the additional filtering options, limit the "Publication Type" to ALR. (Hint: After checking the box for "ALR," you may need to click "Apply Filters.") This will limit the display to A.L.R. Annotations. (Hint: Be sure the "Sort by" drop-down menu is set to "Relevance.") Review the search results. (Notice that the annotation relating to negligence that you located for Question B1, above, also appears in these search results.) Provide the author, title, and citation of an annotation on health maintenance organizations and their liability for negligence of member physicians.

2. Because Westlaw aggregates sources in the search results, you can also find treatise entries on the subject you are researching. Using the filtering options, undo the filter limiting the display to A.L.R. Annotations, and scroll down to select the option to filter your results by "Publication Name." From the list, enter or select "New York Practice Series Publications" and apply it as the filter. Review the filtered search results, and locate a section of the treatise that deals with "Vicarious liability of hospitals, clinics, medical professionals and HMOs." Review the section of the treatise, and answer the following questions:

   a. Do new rules apply to impose vicarious liability simply because a person is a medical professional?

   b. What must there be in order to impose vicarious liability upon a hospital for the malpractice of another physician or health care professional?

III. Lexis

A. Locating Legal Periodicals Using Word Searches

Although this question directs you to use Lexis, you can also locate legal periodicals in Westlaw.

The material you have located so far provides some information about vicarious liability and respondeat superior, but you clearly need more. You decide to research legal periodicals to learn more. In particular, you want to learn more about problems in applying vicarious liability and respondeat superior to medical malpractice cases.

One way to locate legal periodicals is through word searches. To do so you will first want to narrow the scope of the search to Secondary Materials. Go to the main Lexis search screen, and set the filter for "Secondary Materials" (in the "Content Type" tab). After setting a filter for Secondary Materials, search for:

vicarious liability and medical malpractice

Narrow those search results to only Law Reviews and Journals. (Hint: Use the "Narrow By" menu, and click "Law Reviews and Journals" under "Category.")

1. Browse the search results (sorting by "Relevance"), and locate a 2010 article in the *Quinnipiac Health Law Journal*. Click on the link to the article. Provide the full citation to the article.

2. According to the Introduction, what can widespread acceptance of the apparent agency doctrine lead to?

B. Locating Restatements of the Law Using Word Searches

Although this question directs you to use Lexis, you can also locate Restatements in Westlaw.

You would like to continue your research into vicarious liability and respondeat superior. You decide to research Restatements to see if they offer any new information on when an employer is liable for an employee acting within the scope of employment.

Browse Sources by clicking the "Browse" button near the top of the screen and clicking "Sources." Click "By Category" and "Secondary Materials." Search for "Restatement of the Law, Agency 3d—Official Text" using the "Search Within Sources" box (or scroll down under the "R" choices). From the drop-down menu to the right of "Restatement of Law, Agency 3d—Official Text" add this source as a search filter. Now execute the following search:

respondeat superior and vicarious liability and scope of employment

1. Provide the number of the Restatement section that discusses an employee acting within the scope of employment.

2. Click on the link for this Restatement section. When you conduct a word search, one way to locate relevant information within a document is by using the navigation box and arrows at the top of the screen to locate to your search terms within the document. The navigation function, which is available in both Lexis and Westlaw, allows you to jump to the portion of the document where the search terms appear. To use this function, select your navigation terms in the drop-down box and click on the up or down arrow to move through your document.

Select "respondeat superior" from the drop-down navigation menu. Click the down arrow until you see the sentence: "In contrast, respondeat superior subjects an employer to vicarious liability for employee torts committed within the scope of employment, distinct from whether the employer is subject to direct liability." Under this doctrine, what enables the employer to take measures to reduce the incidence of tortious conduct?

C.   Researching Other Secondary Sources

The red search box in Lexis allows you to search all content without specifying a database. As you have just seen, the search results can be limited by type of authority, jurisdiction, or practice area or topic. Without these limits, however, the search will retrieve many types of authority (statutes, cases, secondary sources, etc.).

Continue your research on vicarious liability and respondeat superior and medical malpractice. Using the drop-down menu to the right of your search terms in the red search box limit the "Category" to "Secondary Materials." (Hint: Be sure to delete any other "Narrow By" filters.) Enter the following terms in the red search box and execute the search:

respondeat superior and vicarious liability and medical malpractice

1.   Use the Narrow By options to view Practice Guides. (Hint: Look in the "Category" tab.) Further narrow your results by selecting the LexisNexis Practice Guide on Illinois Personal Injury Litigation and locating the section dealing with "Vicarious Liability." Click on the section title to view the full text of the section. Locate the heading for "Apparent Agency" and the subsection below it for "Apparent Agency Applicable to Hospitals." According to the Illinois Supreme Court in *Gilbert*, what three elements must a plaintiff establish in order to hold a hospital liable under the doctrine of apparent authority?

2.   Return to the search results list. View the Web results the search retrieved. Click on the link to one of the sites in the search results, and review the content. Provide the name of the site you selected. Is the site you viewed a source you would cite in a legal document? Explain why or why not.

IV.   Subscription Databases for Legal Periodicals

Having examined several secondary sources, you now would like to research the most recent scholarly writing on vicarious liability and respondeat superior. Law review articles are a good place to look for the latest writing on topics like these.

You can use Westlaw and Lexis to locate law review articles (as you did above). You can also use subscription services available through your law school library to locate law review articles. Popular subscription services include HeinOnline, LegalTrac, and the Index to Legal Periodicals (or "ILP"). This exercise directs you to use ILP. LegalTrac may be used if your library does not subscribe to ILP.

From your library's portal, locate the Index to Legal Periodicals. (Hint: If you have access to more than one database, choose Index to Legal Periodicals–Full Text.) Click on the link to the Index to Legal Periodicals or follow any other instructions on your library's portal to access the service. Choose the option for "Advanced Search." Enter the following search phrase in the first search box as a Text search:

vicarious liability and respondeat superior and medical malpractice

Execute the search by clicking the "Search" button. Find a 2008 article in the *Wake Forest Law Review*. Click on the PDF Full Text, and answer the following questions.

A. Provide the title of the article.

B. Browse the first two paragraphs of the article. Briefly, according to the article, what did the North Carolina Court of Appeals hold in *Diggs v. Novant Health, Inc.*?

C. Briefly, according to the article, how does the patient see the hospital, and what is the reality?

Exercise 3.1
Researching Secondary Sources Online
with Table of Contents and Word Searches

Name: _____   Due Date: _____

Professor: _____   Section: _____

I.   Review Questions

A.

B.

C.

II.   Westlaw

A.   Searching a Legal Encyclopedia Using the Table of Contents

A.1.

A.2.

A.3.

A.4.

B.   Locating A.L.R. Annotations Using Word Searches

B.1.

B.2.

B.3.

B.4

C.   Researching Multiple Secondary Sources

C.1.

C.2.a.

C.2.b.

III.   Lexis

A.   Locating Legal Periodicals Using Word Searches

A.1.

A.2.

B.　Locating Restatements of the Law Using Word Searches

B.1.

B.2.

C.　Researching Other Secondary Sources

C.1.

C.2.

IV.   Subscription Databases for Legal Periodicals

A.

B.

C.

Exercise 3.2
Researching Legal Encyclopedias and A.L.R. Annotations

Learning Outcomes

After completing this exercise, you should be able to

1. Use secondary sources to gain background information about a legal issue and to locate citations to primary authorities relevant to the issue.

2. Use the organization, features, finding tools, and updating tools in legal encyclopedias and A.L.R. Annotations to conduct research using these resources.

Instructions

1. An answer sheet is provided at the end of the questions for your convenience while you are working on the exercise. After you finish your research, submit your answers in typewritten form on a separate answer sheet. Do not retype the questions. Your answer sheet should contain only the answers to the questions.

2. If you spend more than 15 minutes trying to find the answer to any individual question, use the troubleshooting hints in the General Instructions for this Workbook. If you are still unable to find the answer, stop and seek assistance.

3. The questions in this exercise are designed for you to complete online or in print. Your professor will tell you which resources (Westlaw, Lexis, or the books in your library) to use.

4. If you are researching in print, reshelve all books as soon as you finish using them.

Problem Sets

A   B   C   D   E   F   G   H   I   J   K   L   M   N   O

THE ASSIGNMENT

In this exercise, the supervising attorney in your office has approached you about the client matter for your problem set and has asked you to research it. To do so, you need to research secondary sources to obtain background information and citations to relevant primary authorities. This exercise will guide you through two commonly-used secondary sources to obtain the information you need: legal encyclopedias and American Law Reports (A.L.R.) Annotations. As you conduct your research, you will need to answer questions about the information you find in each source.

Review the client matter for your problem set. This client matter involves a complex area of law. Given the complexity of the subject and amount of authority you are likely to find, secondary sources are a good starting point for your research. They will provide you with the background and history of the subject and will refer you to relevant primary authorities.

You can complete the problems in this exercise online or in print. (Note that Westlaw and Lexis both contain American Jurisprudence 2d and A.L.R., but only Westlaw contains Corpus Juris Secundum.) Your professor will tell you which resources to use. Follow the instructions below for your assigned source (Westlaw, Lexis, or the books in your library).

Client Matter

Problem Set A	You work for an advocacy organization that promotes openness and transparency in government in matters of national security. As part of your work, you seek certain government documents and records through the Freedom of Information Act (or "FOIA"). You need to research government obligations to release information to the public under the FOIA.
Problem Set B	You work for a lobbying organization interested in protecting communities from development of obscene and indecent adult entertainment establishments. Your supervisor has asked you to find information on the constitutional limitations of regulating these establishments.
Problem Set C	You represent a major U.S. drug company. The company is planning to market a new drug and wants to protect itself from products liability lawsuits. The company has asked you how statements it makes in its advertising could affect any products liability claims against it.
Problem Set D	You advise the state Department of Mental Health. The Department is concerned about the liability of hospitals and hospital employee liability when hospitals admit individuals with a mental illness against their will. You need to research law related to involuntary commitment of individuals with a mental illness or condition.
Problem Set E	You work for a non-profit organization interested in protecting the rights of persons accused of crimes. Your supervisor has asked you to research constitutional limitations on the ability of government agents to stop and frisk individuals based on a drug courier profile.
Problem Set F	Your client was falsely arrested and improperly detained by security guards for allegedly shoplifting goods from a department store. He now wishes to sue the guards for punitive and exemplary damages. You need to research the circumstances under which your client may receive punitive or exemplary damages.
Problem Set G	You advise the state Unemployment Compensation Board. The Board is considering adopting new regulations denying unemployment compensation to individuals who commit misconduct outside the workplace. The chairperson of the Board asks for advice. You need to research the law of unemployment compensation, with particular reference to qualifications for unemployment compensation.

Problem Set H	You work for the state police. Your supervisor has asked you to research employment discrimination in police forces in order to design uniform policies to help the state police avoid illegal discrimination in the future.
Problem Set I	You represent the plaintiff in an automobile injury case. You need to research whether your client can collect for pain and suffering as a result of her injuries.
Problem Set J	You are counsel to the state legislative committee with responsibility for elections, voting, campaign finance, and similar issues. The chair of the committee has asked you for a briefing book on laws prohibiting felons and ex-felons from voting. You need to research felon disenfranchisement.
Problem Set K	Your client saw her employer dump toxic waste in an illegal manner. She reported the information to state authorities. The next day, she was fired from her job. You need to research whether she has a valid cause of action against her former employer for wrongful discharge under state whistleblower protections.
Problem Set L	Your client quit her job three years ago to care for her mother, who suffered from Alzheimer's disease. Your client's mother recently died, and your client has learned that she was cut out of her mother's will. She wants to challenge the validity of the will, which was executed while her mother was ill. You need to learn what evidence would be necessary to show that Alzheimer's disease affected your client's mother's capacity to execute the will (and thus the validity of the will).
Problem Set M	You work for a non-profit organization that promotes consumer rights. You are particularly interested in consumer protection laws as they relate to non-English speakers and individuals for whom English is a second language. You need to research consumer protection laws in general, as well as their effects on these individuals.
Problem Set N	You work for the public defenders office. Your client is a juvenile who was convicted of delinquency without the benefit of a lawyer. You are appealing her conviction. Part of your claim is that she did not receive her constitutional right to counsel at her trial and that she did not validly waive that right. You need to research these issues.
Problem Set O	You represent the mother of two young children in a custody dispute with the children's father. You need to research the factors that courts use to award custody and to change custody between biological parents.

I.   Review Questions

A.   Would you be most likely to begin your research on a topic about which you knew very little with a legal encyclopedia or an A.L.R. Annotation? Explain your answer.

B.   Would you be most likely to use a legal encyclopedia or an A.L.R. Annotation to research the law of multiple jurisdictions? Explain your answer.

C. Which of the following statements is false? (a) C.J.S. and Am. Jur. 2d are national encyclopedias that contain references to cases from across the country; (b) state-specific encyclopedias contain references to cases from an individual state; (c) A.L.R. Annotations address only questions of state law, not federal law.

II.   Researching by Citation in Legal Encyclopedias

One resource that can be a useful starting point for a research project is a legal encyclopedia. Legal encyclopedias simply report on the state of the law in a very general way. They are helpful for obtaining general background information on your research topic and for locating limited citations to primary legal authority.

This section requires you to locate material in a legal encyclopedia from a citation. You can locate material by citation online or in print.

A.   Retrieving a Source by Citation

Identify the legal encyclopedia and citation assigned to your problem set in the chart below. Using only the citation, retrieve your assigned section.

If you are researching online, simply type the encyclopedia abbreviation and citation into the search box to retrieve the section assigned for your problem set. For example, for Problem Set A, type the following into the search box:

Am. Jur. 2d Freedom of Information Acts 55

If you are researching in print, locate the appropriate topic in the main volumes of the encyclopedia assigned to your problem set, and turn to the assigned section.

Problem Set	Encyclopedia	Citation
Problem Set A	Am. Jur. 2d	Freedom of Information Acts § 55
Problem Set B	C.J.S.	Obscenity § 12
Problem Set C	Am. Jur. 2d	Products Liability § 860
Problem Set D	C.J.S.	Mental Health § 49
Problem Set E	Am. Jur. 2d	Searches and Seizures § 89
Problem Set F	C.J.S.	Damages § 242
Problem Set G	Am. Jur. 2d	Unemployment Compensation § 68
Problem Set H	C.J.S.	Civil Rights § 240
Problem Set I	Am. Jur. 2d	Damages § 213
Problem Set J	C.J.S.	Elections § 47

Problem Set	Encyclopedia	Citation
Problem Set K	Am. Jur. 2d	Wrongful Discharge § 116
Problem Set L	C.J.S.	Wills § 750
Problem Set M	Am. Jur. 2d	Consumer and Borrower Protection § 278
Problem Set N	C.J.S.	Criminal Procedure and Rights of Accused § 680
Problem Set O	Am. Jur. 2d	Divorce and Separation § 851

Read the section, and answer the Legal Encyclopedia Questions assigned to your problem set in the chart below.

Legal Encyclopedia Questions

Problem Set A	1. Does the FOIA make distinctions based on who is requesting the information?	2. Under the FOIA, each agency must make nonexempt records available to any person who requests them if the request is made properly. In making any record available to a person, an agency must provide the record in what form or format?
Problem Set B	1. A publication must have certain characteristics to be obscene under the principles enunciated by the United States Supreme Court. What are those characteristics?	2. How may a state not define obscenity?
Problem Set C	1. Name two types of advertising statements that may serve as a basis for imposing liability for negligent misrepresentation on a defendant seller or manufacturer, or in other words, are actionable.	2. When is there no cause of action against a manufacturer of a product based on that manufacturer's advertising?
Problem Set D	1. What are the goals of civil commitment or confinement?	2. What are the two legal foundations or justifications for the exercise of authority to confine the mentally ill?
Problem Set E	1. What does an investigatory or *Terry* stop usually involve?	2. What level of suspicion must an investigatory stop be supported by?
Problem Set F	1. What is to be considered in determining whether exemplary damages will be awarded?	2. What must be the justification of punitive damages?

Problem Set G	1. What is the basic principle at the root of an unemployment compensation statute?	2. What types of acts constitute misconduct warranting denial of unemployment compensation?
Problem Set H	1. Under what conditions may an employer give and act upon the results of an ability test for job applicants?	2. When does a test have a disparate impact?
Problem Set I	1. According to this section, "pain and suffering" has served as a convenient label for several specific conditions. List two of these conditions.	2. Under what conditions may pain and suffering be psychosomatic in origin?
Problem Set J	1. Under what circumstances did a provision disenfranchising persons convicted of crimes involving moral turpitude violate the Equal Protection Clause?	2. What purpose do felon disenfranchisement laws serve?
Problem Set K	1. What must a plaintiff demonstrate under some states' acts to establish a prima facie case of retaliatory discharge under the whistleblower statute?	2. What must the court look at to determine whether an employee's report of a violation or suspected violation of law is made in good faith for purposes of a state whistleblower statute?
Problem Set L	1. What type of evidence may be sufficient to carry the issue of testamentary capacity to the jury?	2. Does evidence that relates only to the testator's physical condition compel a conclusion of unsoundness of mind?
Problem Set M	1. Under an unfair-trade practices act, when is an act "unfair"?	2. Generally when is a transaction not unfair?
Problem Set N	1. What are the purposes of the constitutional guarantee of the right to effective assistance of counsel?	2. To whom does the right to counsel belong?
Problem Set O	1. In some jurisdictions, under what conditions do courts give a preference to the mother in custody disputes?	2. In many jurisdictions, there is no prima facie presumption in favor of the mother. In those jurisdictions, what consideration are the parents to receive for custody of a minor child?

1. Answer the first legal encyclopedia question for your problem set.

2. Answer the second legal encyclopedia question for your problem set.

B. If you are researching in print, update your research by checking the pocket part for the main volume. (If you are using Westlaw or Lexis, simply enter "not applicable" as your answer.) Does the pocket part contain any additional information? If so, provide the name of a case or other resource cited in the pocket part. If not, answer "None." (Hint: Volumes published within the past year will not have pocket parts. If the volume you use is too new to have a pocket part, answer "None.")

III.   Researching by Word Search or Index in A.L.R. Annotations

American Law Reports, or A.L.R., Annotations collect summaries of cases, typically from a variety of jurisdictions, to provide an overview of the law on a narrow topic. Unlike legal encyclopedias, which usually focus on very broad topics, A.L.R. Annotations tend to focus on narrower legal questions. A.L.R. Annotations are also more detailed than legal encyclopedia entries because they include summaries of specific cases. Like encyclopedia entries, however, they do not contain much analysis. They simply report the results of decisions. A.L.R. Annotations can be a helpful way to begin your legal research to give you an overview of your research topic as well as providing authorities on both sides of an issue. They can also direct you to primary authority from the controlling jurisdiction and persuasive authority from other jurisdictions.

This section directs you to research A.L.R. Annotations using a word search (online) or an index search (in print).

If you are searching online, you will use bold terms to form a word search to retrieve relevant annotations.

In Westlaw: From the "All Content" tab, follow the links to "Secondary Sources" and click on American Law Reports. Click on "Advanced," enter the **bold** terms and phrases in the "Title" box separated by "and," and execute the search. Sort by relevance. (For example, in Problem Set A you would enter: records and agency and Freedom of Information Act.)

In Lexis: From the Explore Content menu and the "Content Type" tab, select "Secondary Materials" and then click on "American Law Reports (ALR)." Enter the **bold** terms and phrases in the "Title" box separated by "and" and execute the search. Sort by relevance. (For example, in Problem Set A you would enter: records and agency and Freedom of Information Act.)

Locate the A.L.R. Annotation with a title that most closely corresponds to the search terms for your problem set.

If you are researching in print, locate the A.L.R. Index in your library. Use the search terms assigned for your problem set to locate the citation to an A.L.R. Annotation in the A.L.R. Index. Retrieve the Annotation from the main A.L.R. volumes.

Problem Set	A.L.R. Search Terms
Problem Set A	Freedom of Information Acts; Agency records; what are "**records**" of **agency** which must be made available under **Freedom of Information Act** (5 U.S.C.A. § 522(a)(3))
Problem Set B	Lewdness, Indecency, and Obscenity; Zoning; validity of ordinances restricting **location** of "**adult entertainment**" or sex-oriented businesses
Problem Set C	Products Liability; Advertising; statements in **advertisements** as affecting **liability** of manufacturers or sellers for injury caused by product other than **tobacco**
Problem Set D	Incompetent or Insane Persons; Civil rights and discrimination; commitment, right to relief under Federal **Civil Rights** Act of 1871 (42 U.S.C.A. § 1983) for alleged wrongful **commitment** to or confinement in mental **hospital**
Problem Set E	Drugs and Narcotics; courier profile; testimony, admissibility of **drug** courier **profile** testimony in criminal prosecution
Problem Set F	Punitive Damages; Malice; false imprisonment and arrest, defendant's state of mind necessary or sufficient to warrant award of **punitive damages** in action for **false arrest** or imprisonment
Problem Set G	Unemployment Compensation; Conduct; off-duty, conduct or activities of employees during **off-duty** hours as misconduct barring **unemployment** compensation benefits
Problem Set H	Age Discrimination; Law enforcement employment, actions under Age **Discrimination** in **Employment** Act (29 U.S.C.A. §§ 621-634) challenging hiring or **retirement** practices in law enforcement employment
Problem Set I	Pain and Suffering; Mental or **psychological** damages, excessiveness or adequacy of **damages** awarded for injuries causing mental or psychological damages
Problem Set J	Elections and Voting; Conviction; voting rights, effect of **conviction** under federal law, or law of another state or country, on right to **vote** or hold public office
Problem Set K	Discharge from Employment or Office; Damages; at-will employment, **damages** recoverable for wrongful discharge of **at-will** employee; excessiveness or **adequacy** or damages under state law
Problem Set L	Wills; **Alzheimer's** disease as affecting testamentary **capacity**
Problem Set M	Trademarks, Tradenames, and Unfair Trade Practices; Consumer protection; **practices** forbidden by state **deceptive** trade practice and **consumer** protection acts, generally
Problem Set N	Attorneys; Children and minors; waiver of right to counsel, validity and efficacy of minor's waiver of right to **counsel**—cases decided since Application of **Gault**, 387 U.S. 1, 87 S. Ct. 1428, 18 L.Ed.2d 527 (1967)
Problem Set O	Custody and Support of Children; Religion and religious societies; **custody** of children, **religion** as factor in child custody cases

A. Provide the title and A.L.R. citation of the Annotation you located.

B. Browse the Annotation, and answer the two A.L.R. Annotation questions below for your problem set.

A.L.R. Annotation Questions

Problem Set A	1. Using the Article Outline or Index for this Annotation, locate the "Summary and comment" section. The United States Supreme Court in *U.S. Dep't of Justice v. Tax Analysts* held that in order for requested materials to qualify as "agency records" for purposes of FOIA, they must meet two conditions. List the two qualifications or conditions.	2. Locate the section dealing with "Personal notes or letters." Why did the Supreme Court in *Kissinger v. Reporters Committee for Freedom of the Press* reject the argument that material acquired the status of agency records when it was removed from White House files and taken to the party's office at the Department of State?
Problem Set B	1. Using the Article Outline or Index for this Annotation, locate the section on "Summary and comment—generally." What dimension is added when zoning regulations exclude a sexually oriented business such as an "X-rated" movie theater or an adult bookstore?	2. Locate the section on "Summary and comment—Practice pointers." What should an adult business client do when a federal forum is desired for the trial of constitutional claims?
Problem Set C	1. Using the Article Outline or Index for this Annotation, locate the section on "Summary and comment—Practice pointers." What question does products liability litigation often present initially?	2. Why is this question critical?
Problem Set D	1. Using the Article Outline or Index for this Annotation, locate the section on "Tort elements: Duty." In *Campbell v. Glenwood*, what did the court say was an essential element in tort liability (and consequently in an action for deprivation of civil rights)?	2. Locate the section on "Background, summary, and comment—Practice Pointers." What does the federal statute 28 U.S.C. § 1343(3) do?
Problem Set E	1. Using the Article Outline or Index, locate the section on "Summary and comment—Generally." What do characteristics of the drug courier profile include?	2. Locate the section on "Summary and comment—Practice pointers." What should defense counsel consider in situations when a drug courier profile is, or may be, admissible in part or for certain purposes?

Problem Set F	1. Using the Article Outline or Index for this Annotation, locate the section on "Summary and comment—generally." Some courts have specifically held that the requisite malice may be inferred from two circumstances. What are those two circumstances?	2. What has been said to warrant an award of punitive damages in an action for false arrest or imprisonment?
Problem Set G	1. Using the Article Outline or Index for this Annotation, locate the section on "Arrests or convictions—Public employees—Benefits allowed." What did the court hold in *Beaty v. City of Idaho Falls*?	2. Locate the "Practice Pointers" section. Why must unemployment security law be liberally construed in many jurisdictions?
Problem Set H	1. Using the Article Outline or Index for this Annotation, locate the section on "Background, summary, and comment—Background." What is an exception to the prohibition on age discrimination against employees or applicants for employment who are between the ages of 40 and 70?	2. Locate the section on "Background, summary, and comment—Practice pointers." What is a preliminary procedural issue of which counsel in an ADEA law enforcement action should be aware?
Problem Set I	1. Using the Article Outline or Index for this Annotation, locate the "Summary and comment—Practice Pointers" section. What is the first step an attorney must take, after determining that the person has a cause of action for personal injuries, and after establishing an attorney-client relationship?	2. Locate the section on "Summary and comment—Preparation for settlement discussions." After an attorney has determined the nature of the client's injuries and the various elements arising out of the injuries and related matters which can be the basis for damages, what is the attorney ready to do?
Problem Set J	1. Using the Article Outline or Index for this Annotation, locate the section on "Convictions under law of another state: Held disqualification." According to the court in *Application of Smith*, what is the purpose of the disqualifying statute?	2. Locate the "Summary and comment—Practice Pointers" section. How may a person convicted of a crime and not allowed to register to vote raise the issue of his qualifications?

Problem Set K	1. Using the Article Outline for this Annotation, locate the "Summary and comment" section. Under exceptions to the at-will doctrine, a remedy is available in most states for wrongful discharge when the employee has engaged in what kind of conduct?	2. What types of damages are available to an employee for wrongful discharge?
Problem Set L	1. Using the Article Outline or Index for this Annotation, locate the section on "Summary and comment—Generally." What does the presence or absence of testamentary capacity determine?	2. Locate the section on "Summary and comment—Practice pointers" section. Which witnesses' testimony can be critical in a case where the testamentary capacity of the testator is questioned because of Alzheimer's disease?
Problem Set M	1. Using the Article Outline or Index for this Annotation, locate the section on "Background, summary, and comment—Generally." The past decade has seen the enactment of myriad state statutes intended to do what?	2. Locate the section on "Background, summary, and comment—Practice pointers." Why is the body of case law considering questions as to what acts or practices violate state deceptive trade practice and consumer protection statutes relatively limited?
Problem Set N	1. Using the Article Outline or Index for this Annotation, locate the section on "Summary and comment—Generally." Which party bears the burden of proof as to a valid waiver?	2. Locate the section on "Summary and comment—Practice Pointers." When may the issue of whether a juvenile was adequately advised of the right to counsel typically be reviewed for the first time?
Problem Set O	1. Using the Article Outline or Index for this Annotation, locate the section dealing with "Consideration of religious factors generally." In custody proceedings involving contests between natural parents of a child, what view have courts held or expressed with respect to religious factors?	2. Locate the section on "Summary and comment—Practice Pointers." Typically, in a custody determination, what does the court assume?

1. Answer the first A.L.R. Annotation question for your problem set.

2. Answer the second A.L.R. Annotation question for your problem set.

C. Locate the table listing the jurisdictions from which the Annotation cites authority. What is the first jurisdiction listed? (Hint: A.L.R. uses a variety of labels on the table listing jurisdictions. It may be called Table of Jurisdictions Represented, Table of Cases, Jurisdictional Table of Cited Statutes and Cases, or something else to that effect.)

D. If you are researching in print, check the pocket part to the main volume to update your research. If you are using Westlaw or Lexis, check "Research References." Does the pocket part or "Research References" list any related A.L.R. Annotations? If so, provide the title and citation of the first Annotation listed. If not, answer "None."

Exercise 3.2
Researching Legal Encyclopedias and A.L.R. Annotations

Name: _____   Due Date: _____

Professor: _____   Section: _____

I.   Review Questions

A.

B.

C.

II.   Researching by Citation in Legal Encyclopedias

A.1.

A.2.

B.

III.   Researching by Word Search or Index in A.L.R. Annotations

A.

B.1.

B.2.

C.

D.

Exercise 3.3
Researching Secondary Sources on Your Own

Learning Outcomes

After completing this exercise, you should be able to

1. Locate a secondary source on a specific area of law to gain information about a legal issue.

2. Use a secondary source to identify primary authority.

Instructions

1. An answer sheet is provided at the end of the questions for your convenience while you are working on the exercise. After you finish your research, submit your answers in typewritten form on a separate answer sheet. Do not retype the questions. Your answer sheet should contain only the answers to the questions.

2. If you spend more than 20 minutes researching the legal question, use the troubleshooting hints in the General Instructions for this Workbook. If you are still unable to find the answer, stop and seek assistance.

Problem Sets

A   B   C   D   E   F

For letters G to O use the top letter above yours in the chart below unless directed otherwise. For example, letter M does problem set A.

A	B	C	D	E	F
G	H	I	J	K	L
M	N	O			

THE ASSIGNMENT

For this exercise, assume that the supervising attorney in your office has asked you to research the client matter set out in your problem set. This client matter involves an area of the law that may be new or unfamiliar to you. Consequently, secondary sources are a good starting point for your research.

Using Westlaw or Lexis, research any secondary source(s) to find the answers to the questions for your problem set.

Client Matter and Legal Question

Problem Set A	**Client Matter:** You work in a medium-size, plaintiff-side personal injury firm. A partner asks you to research the doctrine of *res ipsa loquitur* for use in a potential medical malpractice claim.	**Legal Question:** Briefly, describe the doctrine of *res ipsa loquitur*.
Problem Set B	**Client Matter:** You are a criminal defense attorney. A client has been charged with attempted murder. You need to research the elements of the crime.	**Legal Question:** What are the elements of attempted murder (at common law, or in any jurisdiction)?
Problem Set C	**Client Matter:** You represent a consumer advocacy organization that seeks to sue the manufacturer of household gas detectors, because they do not sufficiently alert to the presence of dangerous gas in homes. You need to research whether your client or its members have a claim for breach of implied warranty of fitness.	**Legal Question:** Briefly, how do you establish a breach of an implied warranty of fitness (for a particular use)?
Problem Set D	**Client Matter:** You work in the counsel's office at a private university. One of the university's employees was involved in a traffic accident with a student, and the student sued. The employee claims that the accident was at least partially the student's fault. You need to research the law of comparative negligence.	**Legal Question:** Briefly, what does comparative negligence mean?
Problem Set E	**Client Matter:** You work in the office of the state's attorney. Your boss asked you to prepare an indictment against an individual for felony murder. You need to research the elements of felony murder.	**Legal Question:** What does the prosecution need to prove in order to get a conviction for felony murder (at common law, or in any jurisdiction)?
Problem Set F	**Client Matter:** You represent low-income tenants in rental-housing disputes with their landlords. Some of your clients wish to withhold rental payments, because their landlords have not completed necessary improvements to make their units fully habitable. You need to research the law of implied warranty of habitability.	**Legal Question:** Briefly, what is the implied warranty of habitability? Can your clients withhold their rent payments (in any jurisdiction) if their units are not in a habitable condition?

I.   Provide the name and citation of at least one, but no more than three, secondary sources you consulted to find the answer to the legal question. Describe how you located each source.

II.   Answer the legal question.

III. Provide the name and citation of a primary authority cited in the secondary source(s) you consulted that support your answer to Question II, above.

Exercise 3.3
Researching Secondary Sources on Your Own

Name: _____   Due Date: _____

Professor: _____   Section: _____

Problem Set: _____

I.

II.

III.

Chapter 4
CASE RESEARCH

Exercise 4.1
Researching Cases Online with Word Searches

Learning Outcome

After completing this exercise, you should be able to research cases online using word searches.

Instructions

1. An answer sheet is provided at the end of the questions for your convenience while you are working on the exercise. After you finish your research, submit your answers in typewritten form on a separate answer sheet. Do not retype the questions. Your answer sheet should contain only the answers to the questions.

2. If you spend more than 15 minutes trying to find the answer to any individual question, use the troubleshooting hints in the General Instructions for this Workbook. If you are still unable to find the answer, stop and seek assistance.

There are no separate problem sets for this exercise.

THE ASSIGNMENT

For this exercise, you will conduct case research using online resources. You can research cases online in a variety of ways. Three common search techniques are: (1) retrieving a case from its citation; (2) searching by subject area; and (3) executing a word search. Exercise 1.2, Introduction to Online Research, illustrates how to retrieve a case from its citation. Exercise 4.2 covers searching by subject area. This exercise focuses on word searching with Lexis, Bloomberg Law, and Internet sources. Virtually every online source for cases, including Westlaw, allows word searching.

When you retrieve cases online, often you will see symbols next to the case citations, including red or yellow flags in Westlaw and red stop signs or yellow triangles in Lexis. You will learn about these symbols when you learn about a research tool called a citator. In this Workbook, citators are covered in Chapter 5, Research with Citators.

I. Review Questions

A. Are headnotes added by publishers at the beginning of a case ever authoritative?

B. Assume you located a case reported in F.3d. Which of the following statements about this case is true? (1) The case was decided by a federal court. (2) The case was decided by a trial court. (3) The case was decided by a state court.

C. Assume you located a case reported in Fed. Appx. Which of the following statements about this case is false? (1) The case was decided by a federal court. (2) The case was decided by a trial court. (3) The case is nonprecedential.

II.   Legal Question

Your client has come to you with the following problem:

Your client, Sanford Millstein, lives in a small condominium complex in Waterbury, Vermont. He keeps Madagascar Hissing Cockroaches as pets. Although the insects are unusual pets, Mr. Millstein names them and cares deeply for them. Mr. Millstein's next-door neighbor, Shania Westerfeld, does not like the cockroaches. She says she can hear them hissing and is generally uncomfortable with having cockroaches housed in the unit next to hers. She has told Mr. Millstein that, given the opportunity, she would "kill all of those disgusting bugs" he keeps. One day, Mr. Millstein left the screened top covering the tank he uses to house the insects slightly ajar. Two of his favorite insects escaped. Mr. Millstein asked Ms. Westerfeld to keep an eye out for them and to tell him if she saw them so he could recapture them. As it happened, the insects found their way into Ms. Westerfeld's unit. When she discovered them, she killed them immediately, and then told Mr. Millstein what had happened. Mr. Millstein is extremely distraught over the situation and has contacted you to find out if he has a valid claim against Ms. Millstein.

III.   Word Searching in Online Databases

To conduct a word search in most legal research services, you enter a search in the search box. You do not have to specify any filters before you conduct your search; but you have the option to limit the results by type of authority, jurisdiction, practice area, or topic. Without at least some limits, the search will retrieve many types of authority (statutes, cases, secondary sources, etc.). The advantage to this approach is that it allows you to retrieve multiple forms of authority in a single search. When you are not sure what type of authority will help you answer a research question, or when you know you need multiple types of authority, a global search can be effective. The disadvantage is that having all results in a single search may make it difficult to focus on the most relevant or most authoritative sources. You must evaluate the results carefully to make sure you locate and use the best authority available to resolve your research issue.

A. Lexis

To conduct a word search in Lexis, enter a search in the red search box.

For this part of the assignment, you will research two common law issues; therefore, your search results will be limited to cases. One possible claim Mr. Millstein could raise under Vermont law is conversion of personal property because pets are normally treated as the owner's property. But the damages for this type of claim are likely to be low because the value of each cockroach is roughly $2-3. You need to research whether Mr. Millstein can recover either for the emotional distress he has suffered as a result of the loss of his pets or punitive damages.

Using the filters in Lexis, limit the search to Vermont Supreme Court cases. (Hints: Click the tab for "State." Select "Vermont" and then select "VT Supreme Court Cases from 1826.")

Execute the search below by entering the terms in the red search box at the top of the screen (not in any of the other search boxes).

damages conversion property

Sort the search results by relevance, and review results.

1. Provide the name and citation of a case decided by the Vermont Supreme Court in 1986 regarding the sale of a truck that addresses damages for conversion generally and entitlement to punitive damages. (Hint: You can narrow the search results with the filters on the left side of the screen to search for 1986 cases using the "Timeline.")

2. Review the case. What is the measure of damages for conversion generally, and under what circumstances will punitive damages be awarded?

3. Return to your search results. Filters on the left side of the screen enable you to narrow your results. Be sure that you filter only for Vermont Supreme Court cases and not by date. Filter the results of your search further by searching for specific terms within the search results. In the Search within Results search box, enter the following search terms:

"pets" or cat or dog

Execute the search, and review the search results.

a. Provide the names and citations of three cases summarized in the search results that discuss conversion of a pet or other animal.

b. Based on your research, analyze briefly whether your client is likely to be able to recover either noneconomic (emotional distress) or punitive damages for conversion of his pet cockroaches. (Hint: Base your analysis only on the research you have done so far; do not conduct additional research into recoverable damages.)

B. Bloomberg Law

To conduct a word search in Bloomberg Law, enter a search in the <GO> search box in the top right corner of the screen, or choose the option to search "All Legal Content."

For this part of the assignment, assume that Mr. Millstein's claim arises in Alaska. You now need to research Alaska law. Specifically, you need to determine whether Mr. Millstein might be able to pursue a claim of intentional infliction of emotional distress based on Ms. Westerfeld's actions.

From the Bloomberg Law home page, choose the option to search "State Law," and then select Alaska. Enter the search below in the "Keywords" search box:

"emotional distress" /p pet or animal

Options for filtering the search results appear on the left. Because the search was not pre-filtered by type of authority, the results are not limited to cases (which Bloomberg Law calls court opinions).

1. Use the filtering options to limit the results to "Court Opinions" from Alaska. Review the search results. Would an Alaska court recognize a claim for intentional infliction of emotional distress resulting from the loss of a pet? Provide the name and citation (as it appears in Bloomberg Law) for at least one case to support your answer.

2. If Mr. Millstein were to proceed with a claim of intentional infliction of emotional distress, what threshold determinations would the trial court make? Provide the names and citations (as they appear in Bloomberg Law) for two cases to support your answer.

IV. Internet

Many cases are available on the Internet. Depending on the source you use to search, you may be able to search by date, citation, or party name. Some sites also permit word searches. One source for Internet case research is Google Scholar.

Another possible claim Mr. Millstein might assert is negligent infliction of emotional distress if Ms. Westerfeld's actions were negligent rather than intentional. For this part of the assignment, access Google Scholar to research whether Vermont would allow him to recover for negligent infliction of emotional distress based on the destruction of his pets. (Hint: You can access Google Scholar from the main Google search engine page or at scholar.google.com.)

Select the "Case law" button under the search box and check Vermont state courts. Enter the following search in the search box:

negligence and "emotional distress" and pet

Execute the search. Review the search results.

A. Provide the name and citation of a 2009 case in which the court discussed a negligent infliction of emotional distress (NIED) claim based on the death of pet cats.

B. Review the case. What must the plaintiff show to make out a prima facie case for NIED?

C. Based on your review of this case, is Mr. Millstein likely to succeed with an NIED claim? Why or why not?

Exercise 4.1
Researching Cases Online with Word Searches

Name: _____   Due Date: _____

Professor: _____   Section: _____

I.   Review Questions

A.

B.

C.

II.   Legal Question

(There are no questions to answer for this portion of the exercise.)

III.   Word Searching in Online Databases

A.   Lexis

A.1.

A.2.

A.3.a.

A.3.b.

B.   Bloomberg Law

B.1.

B.2.

IV.   Internet

A.

B.

C.

Exercise 4.2
Researching Cases by Subject or Topic

Learning Outcomes

After completing this exercise, you should be able to

1. Describe the coverage and organization of the West Key Number System.

2. Locate case summaries in a print digest or online using the headnotes in a case on point.

3. Search topics in the West Key Number System on Westlaw or the Descriptive Word Index of a digest.

Instructions

1. An answer sheet is provided at the end of the questions for your convenience while you are working on the exercise. After you finish your research, submit your answers in typewritten form on a separate answer sheet. Do not retype the questions. Your answer sheet should contain only the answers to the questions.

2. If you spend more than 15 minutes trying to find the answer to any individual question, use the troubleshooting hints in the General Instructions for this Workbook. If you are still unable to find the answer, stop and seek assistance.

3. This exercise is tailored for online research, but you should also be able to complete the research with print resources. If you use print resources and are unable to find the answer to any individual question within 15 minutes, remember to refer to the troubleshooting hints in the General Instructions or seek assistance.

4. Although some questions include hints reminding you to update your research, others do not. Do not forget to update your research in all sources even if the question does not prompt you to do so.

5. If you complete this exercise using print sources, reshelve all books as soon as you finish using them.

Problem Sets

A B C D E F G H I J K L M N O P Q R

THE ASSIGNMENT

One way to locate cases is to search by subject. The West Key Number System is one of the most commonly used resources for researching cases by subject. For this part of the exercise you must use either Westlaw or print West reporters and digests. Other online services, including Lexis and Bloomberg Law, also allow subject searching, but the problems in this part of the exercise are keyed to the West Key Number System.

This exercise presents two issues for you to research using the West Key Number System. The first issue requires you to use a case on point as a vehicle for locating summaries of additional cases relevant to your research. The second issue requires you to use Westlaw or the digest index to locate cases. This exercise will guide you through the research process. As you conduct your research, you will need to provide answers to the legal question for your problem set. Answer the questions using the cases you locate; do not conduct additional research.

I.   Review Questions

A.   Explain the difference between a digest and a reporter.

B.   Explain the difference between a key number and a headnote.

C.   What is the highest numbered topic in the West Key Number System and what subject does it cover?

II.   Working from a Case on Point

One way to use the digest for case research is to work from a case on point. The West digest topics and Key Numbers are consistent across jurisdictions. Therefore, once you have located a case on point from any jurisdiction, you can use that case as an entry point into the West digest system to research cases from any other jurisdiction.

Your client has approached you about the following situation:

> Your client, Sanford Millstein, lives in a small condominium complex. He keeps Madagascar Hissing Cockroaches as pets and recently began breeding the insects for sale. The insects are kept in tanks. The breeding operation creates no discernable odors, although occasionally the insects' hissing can be heard in the adjoining units. Mr. Millstein's next-door neighbor, Shania Westerfeld, does not like the cockroaches. She is generally uncomfortable with having cockroaches bred in the unit next to hers. The two have had several disputes during which she has told Mr. Millstein that she is "creeped out" by the insects. Ms. Westerfeld complained to the owners' association and the city, but Mr. Millstein is not violating any condominium rule or city ordinance. Despite her requests that he stop breeding cockroaches, he refuses to stop. She has now served him with a complaint alleging private nuisance and requesting both money damages and an injunction to stop his breeding activities. Mr. Millstein has contacted you to find out whether Ms. Westerfeld has a valid nuisance claim.

You need to research the elements, requirements, or definition of a private nuisance claim in the jurisdiction for your problem set.

Jurisdiction

Problem Set A (Kansas)	Problem Set J (South Carolina)
Problem Set B (Texas)	Problem Set K (Nebraska)
Problem Set C (Colorado)	Problem Set L (jurisdiction assigned by your professor; or Iowa if unassigned)
Problem Set D (Connecticut)	Problem Set M (Maryland)
Problem Set E (Ohio)	Problem Set N (Wisconsin)
Problem Set F (jurisdiction assigned by your professor; or Indiana if unassigned)	Problem Set O (Pennsylvania)
Problem Set G (New York)	Problem Set P (Utah)
Problem Set H (Maine)	Problem Set Q (Missouri)
Problem Set I (Mississippi)	Problem Set R (jurisdiction assigned by your professor; or Alabama if unassigned)

Assume that you began your research on this question by reviewing secondary sources and that one of the secondary sources referenced the case listed below for your problem set, which is from another jurisdiction. You can use the topics and Key Numbers in the headnotes from the case listed below to identify similar cases from the jurisdiction for your problem set.

Case On Point

Problem Set	Case On Point
A-F	*City of Aurora v. Navar*, 210 Ill. App. 3d 126, 568 N.E.2d 978 (1991) (discussing *nuisance at common law*)
G-L	*Kreuzer v. George Washington University*, 896 A.2d 238 (D.C. 2006) (discussing the requirements for a *claim of nuisance*)
M-R	*City of Tecumseh v. Deister*, 112 Okla. 3, 239 P. 582 (1925) (discussing *nuisance*)

Look up the case provided, and review the headnotes at the beginning of the case. Use the headnotes to identify a topic and accompanying Key Number related to the potential nuisance claim.

In Westlaw, the Key Number is the subcategory following the key symbol at the beginning of each headnote. This may be a textual phrase or a number, depending on how you view the headnotes. Use the "Change View" option above the headnotes to alternate between the two view options.

In print, the Key Number is the number that follows the key symbol at the beginning of each headnote.

A. Provide the topic and Key Number that seem most relevant to your research. If you are working in Westlaw, you may provide either the textual phrase or the number to answer this question.

   (Hint: Often, multiple topics or Key Numbers will be relevant to an issue you are researching. To research the legal question for your problem set fully, you might research cases under several topics and Key Numbers. This question requires you to identify only one topic and Key Number. Use the terms in italics as a guide to identify the appropriate topic and Key Number for your problem set.)

B. Indicate whether you will access the digest in print or use Westlaw to continue your research.

   If you are working in print, locate the most current series of a digest that summarizes cases from the jurisdiction for your problem set. This may be a state-specific digest or a regional digest, depending on the jurisdiction and your library's holdings.

   Provide the name and, if appropriate, series (e.g., 2d, 3d, 4th) of the digest you used.

C. You can locate relevant case summaries using the topic and Key Number you listed for Question IIA, above, to find relevant cases from the jurisdiction for your problem set.

   In Westlaw, follow three steps:

   (1) Click on the link to the Key Number. (Hint: Again, depending on how the view is set in Westlaw, this link may appear as text following the key symbol. If you see an outline of Key Numbers to the right of the headnote, click on the link to the Key Number itself.)

   (2) When the search results appear, change the jurisdiction to the jurisdiction for your problem set. Be sure to limit the jurisdiction to the appropriate state by unchecking all boxes except the one corresponding to the state for your problem set.

   (3) Review the case summaries.

   In print, look up the topic and Key Number in the main digest volumes and review the case summaries. Then do the same in the pocket part or cumulative supplement. (Hints: The newest cases will be summarized in the pocket part or cumulative supplement. The pocket part or cumulative supplement may or may not list cases from the jurisdiction from your problem set. Main digest volumes that have been reprinted recently may not have pocket parts or cumulative supplements. Conversely, older cases will be summarized in earlier series of the digest set. If no cases appear in the main volume or pocket part for the current digest, use an earlier series for older cases.)

1. Provide the name and citation (as they appear in the digest or Westlaw) for at least two, but no more than three, cases from the state courts in the jurisdiction for your problem set that provide the elements for or definition of a nuisance or private nuisance claim.

   (Hints: If many cases are summarized under the Key Number, limit your review to the first 15 state cases from your jurisdiction. In Westlaw, the results will include federal cases unless you unchecked the box to "Include Related Federal" cases. In print, regional digests may list cases from multiple states, and state digests may list federal cases before cases decided by the state's courts.)

   Look for case summaries that list or describe the requirements of a nuisance or private nuisance claim. If more than one citation for the case appears (e.g., citations for denials of rehearing or certiorari), provide only the first citation.

2. If you conducted research in print, were any of the cases you listed for Question C1, above, summarized in the pocket part or cumulative supplement? If so, list the case(s). If not, answer "no." If you conducted research with Westlaw, answer "not applicable."

D. Look up one case you listed for Question C1, above, in Westlaw or the appropriate print reporter.

1. Briefly describe the facts of the case. (Hint: If the case is long, focus on the facts relevant to nuisance.)

2. Using only this case, explain briefly whether Ms. Westerfeld is likely to be able to show interference with her property sufficient to constitute a nuisance. (Hint: You may not be able to reach a definitive conclusion with the information you have. Make your best assessment using the information you have.)

III. Searching by Topic or Using the Descriptive Word Index

You do not have to locate a case on point to access the digest. You can also search the West Key Number System in Westlaw or use the Descriptive Word Index in print to find relevant topics and Key Numbers. Assume you learned the following new facts about your client's situation:

Mr. Millstein again accidentally left the screened cover off one of the tanks holding the insects he was breeding, and several insects escaped. Fearing that they would travel to Ms. Westerfeld's unit, Mr. Millstein wanted to enter her unit to look for the insects. He knocked on the door, and when she answered, rushed past her into her unit to look for the insects. He found them and removed them. Ms. Westerfeld has now served Mr. Millstein with an amended complaint that adds a count for trespass to land based on the entry of both the insects and Mr. Millstein into her condominium. You need to find out the elements of a claim for trespass to land.

A. In Westlaw, access the West Key Number System from the "Tools" tab. Set the jurisdiction to the jurisdiction for your problem set (using the links immediately below the search box). Enter the term "Trespass" in the search box and execute the search.

In print, locate the Descriptive Word Index for the digest set you used for Part II, above. Look up "Trespass," focusing on entries involving "real property."

Review the Key Number search results or index entries. You should see a variety of subheadings, most or all of which refer to a single topic. To which topic do the subheadings refer?

B. In Westlaw, review the list of subtopics from the Westlaw Key Number search results. In print, look up the topic you identified for Question A, above, in the digest and review the topic outline.

Which Key Number summarizes cases relating to the Entry requirement for trespass to real property (or land)? (Hint: The Key Number is the number following the key symbol.)

C. In Westlaw, click on the link to the Key Number. In print, locate the case summaries under the topic and Key Number in the digest. Review the case summaries, and provide the information requested below for your problem set. (Hint: More than one case may apply. You only need to list one case. If you are conducting research in print and find no cases, be sure to update your research and, if necessary, consult an earlier series of the digest for summaries of older cases.)

Westlaw Key Number or Digest Question

Problem Set	Question
A	Provide the name and citation of a state case that discusses whether substantial certainty that an entry onto land will occur is sufficient for trespass.
B	Provide the name and citation of a state case that discusses whether the entry of a thing (rather than a person) can constitute a trespass.
C	Provide the name and citation of a state case that discusses how an actor may commit a trespass without entering the land him- or herself.
D	Provide the name and citation of a state case that discusses the nature of the intrusion upon the property necessary for trespass.
E	Provide the name and citation of a state case that explains whether trespass requires that the property owner suffer harm.
F	Answer the question provided by your professor. If Indiana, provide the name and citation of a state case that discusses whether release of noxious chemicals can be a trespass.
G	Provide the name and citation of a state case involving trespass caused by toxic chemicals.
H	Provide the name and citation of a state case that explains the gist of a trespass action.
I	Provide the name and citation of a state case that discusses trespass caused by chemical discharges.
J	Provide the name and citation of a state case that discusses whether invasion of land by smoke, noise, light, and vibration is sufficient to constitute a trespass.
K	Provide the name and citation of a state case that discusses entry of a thing beneath the surface of the land.
L	Answer the question provided by your professor. If Iowa, provide the name and citation of a state case that discusses the observable or physical invasion necessary for trespass.
M	Provide the name and citation of a state case that discusses trespass caused by cigarette smoke.
N	Provide the name and citation of a state case that explains what the plaintiff has the burden of showing in a trespass claim.
O	Provide the name and citation of a state case that explains what intent refers to in the context of trespass.
P	Provide the name and citation of a state case that discusses the entry of a thing on the land.
Q	Provide the name and citation of a state case that discusses whether trespass requires damage to be done.
R	Answer the question provided by your professor. If Alabama, provide the name and citation of a state case which discusses whether an entry on land in the possession of plaintiff, actually or constructively, without express or implied authority, is necessary to sustain an action for trespass to realty.

Exercise 4.2
Researching Cases by Subject or Topic

Name: _____   Due Date: _____

Professor: _____   Section: _____

Problem Set: _____

I.   Review Questions

    A.

    B.

    C.

II.   Working from a Case on Point

    A.

B.

C.1.

C.2.

D.1.

D.2.

III.   Searching by Topic or Using the Descriptive Word Index

A.

B.

C.

Exercise 4.3
Researching Cases on Your Own

Learning Outcome

To locate cases to answer a legal question.

Instructions

1. An answer sheet is provided at the end of the questions for your convenience while you are working on the exercise. After you finish your research, submit your answers in typewritten form on a separate answer sheet. Do not retype the questions. Your answer sheet should contain only the answers to the questions.

2. If you spend more than 20 minutes researching the legal question, use the troubleshooting hints in the General Instructions for this Workbook. If you are still unable to find the answer, stop and seek assistance.

3. Do not forget to update your research even though the questions do not prompt you to do so.

4. If you complete this exercise using print sources, reshelve all books as soon as you finish using them.

Problem Sets

A   B   C   D   E   F   G   H   I   J   K   L   M   N   O   P   Q   R

THE ASSIGNMENT

Review the legal question below, and conduct state case law research in the jurisdiction specified in your problem set to determine the answer. (Hint: Make sure that you locate *state* cases—not *federal* cases—to answer the question.)

Unlike the questions in Exercises 4.1 and 4.2 that directed you to specific information, this exercise requires you to conduct and evaluate the results of your research independently. If your professor permits you to choose between print and online research for this exercise, you may want to conduct research both ways to compare your results.

Legal Question

Your client, Annette Parker, purchased a home several years ago that has a treehouse in one of the trees in the back yard. Ms. Parker has no children and paid no attention to the treehouse, which deteriorated into disrepair. Last week, her next-door neighbors had their grandchildren at their house for a visit. One of the children, eight-year-old Madison, wandered into Ms. Parker's back yard without permission and saw the treehouse. She climbed the ladder up to the treehouse. Because the floorboards were rotten, one of them broke as Madison attempted to enter into the treehouse. She fell and was injured and has filed a negligence suit against Ms. Parker. Although Madison trespassed on Ms. Parker's land, the attractive nuisance doctrine may affect Ms. Parker's obligation toward a trespassing child. You need to investigate the following questions: (1) Does your jurisdiction follow the attractive nuisance doctrine? (2) If so, what are the requirements or elements of the doctrine, and if not, what standard of care or duty does a landowner owe to a child trespasser?

Jurisdictions

Problem Set A (Kansas)	Problem Set J (South Carolina)
Problem Set B (Texas)	Problem Set K (Nebraska)
Problem Set C (Colorado)	Problem Set L (jurisdiction assigned by your professor; or Iowa if not assigned)
Problem Set D (Connecticut)	Problem Set M (Maryland)
Problem Set E (Ohio)	Problem Set N (Wisconsin)
Problem Set F (jurisdiction assigned by your professor; or Indiana if not assigned)	Problem Set O (Pennsylvania)
Problem Set G (New York)	Problem Set P (Utah)
Problem Set H (Maine)	Problem Set Q (Missouri)
Problem Set I (Mississippi)	Problem Set R (jurisdiction assigned by your professor; or Alabama if not assigned)

I.   Selecting a Digest, Database, or Research Source

Indicate which print digest or online research source you will use to conduct your research.

II.   Conducting Research

Record all the steps in your research process.

III.   Determining Which Case(s) Apply

Provide the name and citation of at least one case, but no more than three cases, that state (1) whether your jurisdiction follows the attractive nuisance doctrine, and (2) the requirements or elements of the doctrine (if the jurisdiction follows the doctrine) or the standard of care or duty a landowner owes to a child trespasser (if your jurisdiction does not follow the doctrine).

IV.   Answering the Legal Question

Based on the results of your research, list the requirements or elements of the attractive nuisance doctrine (if your jurisdiction follows the doctrine), or state the standard of care or duty a landowner owes to a child trespasser (if your jurisdiction does not follow the doctrine).

Exercise 4.3
Researching Cases on Your Own

Name: _____   Due Date: _____

Professor: _____   Section: _____

Problem Set: _____

I.   Selecting a Digest, Database, or Research Source

II.   Conducting Research

III.   Determining Which Case(s) Apply

IV.   Answering the Legal Question

Chapter 5
RESEARCH WITH CITATORS

Exercise 5.1
Researching Cases with Citators

Learning Outcomes

After completing this exercise, you should be able to

1. Check case citations online using KeyCite in Westlaw, Shepard's in Lexis, and BCite in Bloomberg Law.

2. Interpret citator entries.

3. Understand the differences among Shepard's in Lexis, KeyCite in Westlaw, and BCite in Bloomberg Law.

Instructions

1. An answer sheet is provided at the end of the questions for your convenience while you are working on the exercise. After you finish your research, submit your answers in typewritten form on a separate answer sheet. Do not retype the questions. Your answer sheet should contain only the answers to the questions.

2. If you spend more than 15 minutes trying to find the answer to any individual question, use the troubleshooting hints in the General Instructions for this Workbook. If you are still unable to find the answer, stop and seek assistance.

Problem Sets
A   B   C   D   E

For letters F to R use the top letter above yours in the chart below unless directed otherwise. For example, letter M does problem set C.

A	B	C	D	E
F	G	H	I	J
K	L	M	N	O
P	Q	R		

THE ASSIGNMENT

Once you have located one or more cases relevant to a legal question, the next step in the research process is to use a citator, both to verify the continued validity of the case or cases you have found and to locate additional research references relevant to your legal question. This exercise guides you through the process of using three online citators: KeyCite in Westlaw, Shepard's in Lexis, and BCite in Bloomberg Law. Each of these citators will tell you whether a case is still valid, and each will provide you with additional research references relevant to your legal question. At the same time, these services are not identical: They each contain slightly different information, and they each present information in slightly different ways.

Although you would ordinarily locate a case or cases through other research tools (for example, those covered in the previous chapters) before using a citator, this exercise provides you with the case citation you will use to update your research.

I. Review Questions

A. Which one or more of the following statements is true about a case whose citator entry shows a red stop sign (Shepard's in Lexis), a red flag (KeyCite in Westlaw), or a red box with a negative sign (BCite in Bloomberg Law): (a) the case is no longer valid and cannot be cited for any purpose; (b) the case is no longer valid for at least one of the points it discusses; (c) the case may be valid for one or more of the points it discusses.

B. If you locate a case whose citator entry shows a yellow triangle (Shepard's in Lexis), a yellow flag (KeyCite in Westlaw), or a blue box with a diagonal line (BCite in Bloomberg Law) can you rely on that case as valid without further research? Explain your answer.

C. Shepard's in Lexis, KeyCite in Westlaw, and BCite in Bloomberg Law list the history of a citing case and citing sources that have cited the original case. What is the difference in the way the *citing cases* in these services are organized? Explain your answer. (Hint: You may wish to complete Part II, below, before answering this question.)

II. Using KeyCite, Shepard's, and BCite

A client has come to you with the following legal question:

Your client is Juana Menendez. She lives in an apartment with her two children, Carlos (age four) and Emily (age two). Ms. Menendez's family doctor recently told her that her children have dangerously high levels of lead in their blood. After some investigation, Ms. Menendez discovered that the walls and trim in her apartment unit are painted with lead-based paint. She believes that the lead-based paint in her unit has caused her children to have high levels of lead in their blood. She asks you if she can hold the landlord liable for her children's condition. You need to research whether and how a landlord who uses lead-based paint can be held liable for Carlos's and Emily's condition.

Assume that you located the case listed below for your problem set. You need to find out whether your case is still valid and whether it can lead you to additional cases relevant to your legal question. In the questions below, the phrase "original case" refers to the case listed below, and the phrase "citing sources" refers to sources citing the original case. Locate the original case for your problem set, and answer the questions below.

Original Case

Problem Set A	*Antwuauna A. v. Heritage Mutual Ins. Co.*, 596 N.W.2d 456 (Wis. 1999)
Problem Set B	*Juarez by Juarez v. Wavecrest Management Team Ltd.*, 672 N.E.2d 135 (N.Y. 1996)
Problem Set C	*Gore v. People's Savings Bank*, 665 A.2d 1341 (Conn. 1995)
Problem Set D	*Dunson v. Friedlander Realty*, 369 So. 2d 792 (Ala. 1979)
Problem Set E	*Polakoff v. Turner*, 869 A.2d 837 (Md. 2007)

A.   Checking Case Citations with KeyCite in Westlaw

Using the universal search box in Westlaw, retrieve the case for your problem set. (Hint for Problem Set B: Be sure to view the case in its North Eastern Reporter version, cited above, and not in its New York Official Reports version.)

1. Briefly, in a sentence or two, explain why this case might be relevant to your research.

2. A status flag appears near the caption of the original case. Describe the notation, and explain what it signifies about the case.

3. View the information under the "Negative Treatment" tab. Briefly, in a sentence or two, describe the negative treatment that your case has received.

4. View the "Citing References." Notice that they are organized by cases, trial court orders, secondary sources, and other categories. It is important to pay attention to the type of document in the entry because some have no effect on the continued validity of the citing case (e.g., cases decided by courts outside the controlling jurisdiction or motions filed in related cases), while others may be critical to your understanding of the law in your jurisdiction. Click on "Cases" under the "View" menu on the left side of the screen. In the "Narrow" filters (also on the left side of the screen), open the state jurisdictions. (Hint: Under "Jurisdiction," click on "State.") How many of the cases are from the same state as the original case? (Hint: Look for cases from the state's courts, not cases from the federal courts from the state. The number of cases from each state is listed to the right of each state's name.)

5. KeyCite entries contain references to West headnotes. A headnote summarizes a point of law discussed in the original case. A headnote reference in a KeyCite entry identifies a proposition of law for which a citing source cites the original case. Thus, if a point of law discussed in the original case is summarized in headnote 1, and the KeyCite entry lists a citing case with a reference to headnote 1, you know that the citing case cited the original case for the proposition summarized in headnote 1 of the original case. Headnote references can help you identify authorities that cite the original case on specific issues.

    You can limit the KeyCite display to show only the information most relevant to your research. You want to display state cases from the same state as the original case and then show only cases that cite the original case for the proposition summarized in the headnote listed below for your problem set. To do so, be sure the "Citing References" tab is selected. On the left side limit the "View" to "Cases." Using the "Narrow" options, look under "Jurisdiction" and click open "State" to select the checkbox for state cases from the same state as the original case. Once the state box is checked, look under the "Headnote Topics" to find one matching the topic in bold below and click "specify" to find your headnote number. Check the box for "citing references" and click "Filter results."

Headnote Reference

Problem Set A	Headnote 10	(**Landlord and Tenant** headnote on Walls and paint)
Problem Set B	Headnote 3	(**Landlord and Tenant** headnote on Walls and paint)
Problem Set C	Headnote 3	(**Negligence** headnote on Standard established by statute or regulation)
Problem Set D	Headnote 6	(**Landlord and Tenant** headnote on Walls and paint)
Problem Set E	Headnote 10	(**Landlord and Tenant** headnote on Walls and paint)

The display will be limited to those cases from the same state as the original case with the headnote reference for your problem set.

Click on the link to one of the cases to see what the citing source says about the original case.

Provide the name and citation of the case you selected, and briefly explain what the citing case says about the original case.

(Hints: You may find more than one case from the appropriate jurisdiction that discusses the headnote for your problem set. You can choose any case that discusses the appropriate headnote. It does not matter whether the case also discusses other headnotes.)

6. Go back to the Citing References page. Clear the filters by clicking "Undo Filters." Under "View," select "Secondary Sources" and "ALR." Provide the citation (as it appears in KeyCite) of an ALR Annotation that cites the original case. (Hint: The entry may list more than one ALR Annotation. You only need to provide one citation to answer this question. Do not cite an annotation that has been superseded.)

B.   Checking Case Citations with Shepard's in Lexis

Shepardize the original case for your problem set. (The citations are repeated below.) In the red search box, type "shep:" followed by the citation for the original case for your problem set (e.g., shep: 369 So. 2d 792). Execute the search.

Original Case

Problem Set A	*Antwuauna A. v. Heritage Mutual Ins. Co.,* 596 N.W.2d 456 (Wis. 1999)
Problem Set B	*Juarez by Juarez v. Wavecrest Management Team Ltd.,* 672 N.E.2d 135 (N.Y. 1996)
Problem Set C	*Gore v. People's Savings Bank,* 665 A.2d 1341 (Conn. 1995)
Problem Set D	*Dunson v. Friedlander Realty,* 369 So. 2d 792 (Ala. 1979)
Problem Set E	*Polakoff v. Turner,* 869 A.2d 837 (Md. 2007)

1. A Shepard's signal appears near the case name and citation. Describe the notation and explain what it signifies about the case.

2. Lexis adds headnotes to cases as research references just like West and many official state reporters do. Review the Citing Decisions and identify one or more cases from the same state as the original case with the LexisNexis Headnote reference below for your problem set. To do so, click "Citing Decisions," and in the "Narrow By" options in the left margin click on the headnote number for your problem set. Provide the name and citation of one case from your problem set jurisdiction.

    (Hints: You may find more than one case that discusses the headnote for your problem set. You can choose any case that discusses the headnote. It does not matter whether the case also discusses other headnotes. Be sure to choose a case from the same state as the original case.)

LexisNexis Headnote Reference

Problem Set A	Headnote 4
Problem Set B	Headnote 10
Problem Set C	Headnote 13
Problem Set D	Headnote 2
Problem Set E	Headnote 5

3. If the original case has been cited in secondary sources such as treatises or law review articles, Shepard's will include those sources in the entry. Select "Other Citing Sources" and then narrow to "Law Reviews." Provide the title and citation (as it appears in the Shepard's entry) to the first document in the Shepard's entry.

4. In addition to viewing the full entry, you can customize the display in Shepard's to identify sources that treat the original case in a specific way. Select "Citing Decisions." Use the "Narrow By" options in the left margin to limit the display to cases from the same state as your original case and as indicated below for your problem set. (Hint: Be sure to clear the "Narrow By" option for the LexisNexis Headnote from Question 3, above.)

    Provide the name and citation of a Citing Decision that treats the original case in the manner indicated for your problem set.

    (Hint: You may find more than one case that treats the original case in the manner indicated for your problem set. You only need to list one case in answer to this question.)

Restricted Display Option

Problem Set A	Followed by
Problem Set B	Distinguished by
Problem Set C	Explained by
Problem Set D	Followed by
Problem Set E	Distinguished by

C.   Checking Case Citations with BCite in Bloomberg Law

Retrieve the case for your problem set in Bloomberg Law. The citations are repeated below.

Problem Set A	*Antwuauna A. v. Heritage Mutual Ins. Co.*, 596 N.W.2d 456 (Wis. 1999)
Problem Set B	*Juarez by Juarez v. Wavecrest Management Team Ltd.*, 672 N.E.2d 135 (N.Y. 1996)
Problem Set C	*Gore v. People's Savings Bank*, 665 A.2d 1341 (Conn. 1995)
Problem Set D	*Dunson v. Friedlander Realty*, 369 So. 2d 792 (Ala. 1979)
Problem Set E	*Polakoff v. Turner*, 869 A.2d 837 (Md. 2007)

Bloomberg Law contains a citator that works much like KeyCite in Westlaw and Shepard's in Lexis. (Unlike those services, Bloomberg Law does not have a headnote system for all cases, however.) Bloomberg Law also contains other material not in Westlaw and Lexis, such as docket entries for cases that cite your original case. The tabs across the top of the case provide access to the BCite displays.

1. Open the "Case Analysis" tab. This tab contains a list of all the cases that cite your original case. (You can also open the "Citing Documents" tab and filter your results by "Court Opinions" to get the same list.) Use the "Filter Your Results" options in the left margin to limit the display to those citing cases that have a negative status. (Hint: Under "Citing Case Status," check "Negative.") Provide the name and citation (as it appears in Bloomberg Law) to the earliest (oldest) case listed. (Hint: Be sure the "Sort" drop-down menu is set to "Date (Newest)." The earliest (oldest) case is the one at the bottom of this list.)

2. Open the "Table of Authorities" tab. This tab contains a list of all the cases cited within your original case. How many cases are cited within your original case?

3. Open the "Direct History" tab. Review the direct history of your case by reading the summary or summaries in the numbered box or boxes under the "Direct History Summary" heading. (Hint: The numbered box or boxes include subsequent citations to your case and any earlier and lower-court decisions relating to your case, accompanied by a description of how your case affected those decisions.) Describe the most recent entry in the direct history of your case (affirming, reversing, etc.).

4. Go back to the "Citing Documents" page for your original case. Clear the selected filters. Use the "Filter Your Results" option to limit the display as indicated below for your problem set. What is the title of the earliest (oldest) entry in your results? (Hint: If multiple entries are given and dates are not displayed, give the latest entry listed.)

Restricted Display Option

Problem Set A	Law Reports
Problem Set B	Law Reports
Problem Set C	Jury Instructions
Problem Set D	Books & Treatises
Problem Set E	Books & Treatises

Exercise 5.1
Researching Cases with Citators

Name: _____   Due Date: _____

Professor: _____   Section: _____

Problem Set: _____

I. Review Questions

A.

B.

C.

II.   Using KeyCite, Shepard's, and BCite

A.   Checking Case Citations with KeyCite in Westlaw

A.1.

A.2.

A.3.

A.4.

A.5.

A.6.

B.   Checking Case Citations with Shepard's in Lexis

B.1.

B.2.

B.3.

B.4.

C.   Checking Case Citations with BCite in Bloomberg Law

C.1.

C.2.

C.3.

C.4

Exercise 5.2
Researching Statutes and Secondary Sources with Citators

Learning Outcome

After completing this exercise, you should be able to access and interpret Shepard's, KeyCite, and Bloomberg's Case Analysis entries for statutes and secondary sources.

Instructions

1. An answer sheet is provided at the end of the questions for your convenience while you are working on the exercise. After you finish your research, submit your answers in typewritten form on a separate answer sheet. Do not retype the questions. Your answer sheet should contain only the answers to the questions.

2. If you spend more than 15 minutes trying to find the answer to any individual question, use the troubleshooting hints in the General Instructions for this Workbook. If you are still unable to find the answer, stop and seek assistance.

There are no separate problem sets for this exercise.

THE ASSIGNMENT

Exercise 5.1 shows you how to use Shepard's, KeyCite, and Bloomberg Law in conjunction with case research. This exercise illustrates how to use Shepard's, KeyCite, and Bloomberg Law in conjunction with research on other forms of primary and secondary authority.

I. Shepard's in Lexis

You can use Shepard's to update your research on a statute and to retrieve authority that cites the statute. (You can also use KeyCite and Bloomberg Law to update your research on a statute and retrieve citing sources. Each of these services contains slightly different features and information.) Shepard's provides current information about amendments and other legislative actions affecting the statute's status, as well as citations to cases and other sources citing the statute.

Retrieve the following federal statute in Lexis and answer the questions that follow:

42 USCS § 3604

A. Briefly, in a sentence, explain what the statute prohibits.

B. Shepard's tells you if there is any pending legislation that might affect this statute. Look for an upside-down yellow triangle with an exclamation point, accompanied by the phrase "Pending Legislation," near the top of the page. Is there any pending legislation that might affect this statute? If so, provide the citation to one bill, as it appears in Shepard's.

C. Shepardize the statute by clicking the "Shepardize this document" link in the right margin. The Supreme Court ruled on this statute in 2015. What is the name of the Supreme Court case?

D. Select the option for "Other Citing Sources" in the left margin. Narrow your search results to "Court Documents." The statute is cited in several briefs filed in September 2015 in a case before the U.S. Supreme Court. What is the name of that case?

II. KeyCite in Westlaw

You can use KeyCite in Westlaw to retrieve authorities that cite to secondary authorities. (You can use Shepard's for this purpose, too.) This is useful to locate additional secondary authorities relevant to your research, or to determine whether a particular secondary authority is persuasive to courts in your jurisdiction.

A. Enter the following citation to a law review article in the universal search box in Westlaw:

63 Am. U. L. Rev. 357

1. Provide the author, title, and year of the article.

2. Select the tab for "Citing References." Provide the name of a U.S. Supreme Court case that cites this article.

B. Enter the following citation in the universal search box in Westlaw to locate the provision of the *Restatement (Second) of Agency* addressing "When Master is Liable for Torts of His Servants":

rest 2d agency s 219

1. Briefly, in a sentence, what does this section provide?

2. Provide the name and official citation to a 2003 U.S. Supreme Court case that cites this section. (Hint: Provide the official citation to United States Reports (U.S.).)

3. Briefly, in a sentence, what does this case hold?

C. KeyCite is available for A.L.R. Annotations. Retrieve the following A.L.R. Annotation from its citation and answer the questions below:

100 alr fed 97

1. What is the title of the Annotation?

2. View the Citing References. Provide the name of a 2008 case from Indiana that cites the Annotation.

III. Citations in Bloomberg Law

You can use Bloomberg Law to retrieve authorities that cite to a statute by using the "Smart Code" tab. (You can use Shepard's in Lexis and KeyCite in Westlaw for this purpose, too.) Retrieve the following federal statute in Bloomberg Law, and answer the questions that follow:

42 U.S.C. § 3605

A. Briefly, in a sentence, explain what the statute prohibits.

B. Select the tab for "Smart Code." Using the search filters under "Smart Code Criteria" in the left margin, provide the name and citation of a 2000 case from the United States Court of Appeals for the Seventh Circuit on the Topic of "Damages and Remedies."

Exercise 5.2
Researching Statutes and Secondary Sources with Citators

Name: _____   Due Date: _____

Professor: _____   Section: _____

I.   Shepard's in Lexis

A.

B.

C.

D.

II.   KeyCite in Westlaw

A.1.

A.2.

B.1.

B.2.

B.3.

C.1.

C.2.

III. Citations in Bloomberg Law

A.

B.

Exercise 5.3
Checking Case Citations on Your Own

Learning Outcome

After completing this exercise, you should be able to update case research and locate research references using a citator.

Instructions

1. An answer sheet is provided at the end of the questions for your convenience while you are working on the exercise. After you finish your research, submit your answers in typewritten form on a separate answer sheet. Do not retype the questions. Your answer sheet should contain only the answers to the questions.

2. If you spend more than 20 minutes checking the case citation, use the troubleshooting hints in the General Instructions for this Workbook. If you are still unable to find the answers to the questions, stop and seek assistance.

Problem Sets

A   B   C   D   E   F   G   H   I   J   K   L   M   N   O   P   Q   R

THE ASSIGNMENT

This exercise is related to Exercise 4.3, Researching Cases on Your Own. You will need to use the citation to one of the cases you located in Exercise 4.3 to answer the legal question for your problem set for this exercise. The legal question and problem set jurisdictions are repeated below. If you have not completed Exercise 4.3, your professor will provide you with a citation.

This exercise requires you to use a citator to check the validity of a case and locate research references relevant to an issue discussed in the case. For any citation you use to complete this exercise, you should be able to determine whether the case remains valid. Depending on the case, however, you may or may not find additional research references through the citator. You may find that the case has an extensive history and has been cited numerous times, or you may find that it has never been cited at all.

Legal Question

Your client, Annette Parker, purchased a home several years ago that has a treehouse in one of the trees in the back yard. Ms. Parker has no children and paid no attention to the treehouse, which deteriorated into disrepair. Last week, her next-door neighbors had their grandchildren at their house for a visit. One of the children, eight-year-old Madison, wandered into Ms. Parker's back yard without permission and saw the treehouse. She climbed the ladder up to the treehouse. Because the floorboards were rotten, one of them broke as Madison attempted to enter into the treehouse. She fell and was injured and has filed a negligence suit against Ms. Parker. Although Madison trespassed on Ms. Parker's land, the attractive nuisance doctrine may affect Ms. Parker's obligation toward a trespassing child. You need to investigate the following questions: (1) Does your jurisdiction follow the attractive nuisance doctrine? (2) If so, what are the requirements or elements of the doctrine, and if not, what standard of care or duty does a landowner owe to a child trespasser?

Jurisdictions

Problem Set A (Kansas)	Problem Set J (South Carolina)
Problem Set B (Texas)	Problem Set K (Nebraska)
Problem Set C (Colorado)	Problem Set L (jurisdiction assigned by your professor; or Iowa if not assigned)
Problem Set D (Connecticut)	Problem Set M (Maryland)
Problem Set E (Ohio)	Problem Set N (Wisconsin)
Problem Set F (jurisdiction assigned by your professor; or Indiana if not assigned)	Problem Set O (Pennsylvania)
Problem Set G (New York)	Problem Set P (Utah)
Problem Set H (Maine)	Problem Set Q (Missouri)
Problem Set I (Mississippi)	Problem Set R (jurisdiction assigned by your professor; or Alabama if not assigned)

I.   Locating the Case

Locate the case for your problem set, and review it. Briefly explain why it might be relevant to your research on the legal question. (Hint: The case citation does not appear in this exercise. You should use either one of the citations you located for Exercise 4.3, Researching Cases on Your Own, or a citation provided by your professor.)

II.   Selecting a Citator

Indicate which citator(s) you will use to check the citation.

III.   Using the Citator and Interpreting the Entry

Enter the citation in the citator(s) you have decided to use, and answer the questions below.

A. Determining the Validity of the Case

Is the case still authoritative in the jurisdiction where it was decided for the propositions of law that made it relevant to your research? Explain your answer. (Hint: You may not be able to answer this question solely from the citator entries. You may need to review some of the citing sources to answer this question.)

B. Locating Research References

Although the case you are checking states a rule that is relevant to the legal question, you need to find additional authority to support the rule. Review the citator entry to identify additional cases in your jurisdiction that state the rule you are researching. List up to three cases you could cite for additional support for the rule. If the entry does not list any cases that would provide additional support, answer "No relevant citing cases." An unpublished table disposition or a court order should not be cited. (Hint: Be sure to narrow the scope of the cases you review to only those state cases in your jurisdiction.)

Exercise 5.3
Checking Case Citations on Your Own

Name: _____   Due Date: _____

Professor: _____   Section: _____

Problem Set: _____

I.   Locating the Case

II.   Selecting a Citator

III.   Using the Citator and Interpreting the Entry

A.

B.

Chapter 6
STATUTORY RESEARCH

Exercise 6.1
Researching Statutory Provisions Online

Learning Outcomes

After completing this exercise, you should be able to

1. Locate statutes by using an online index, browsing a table of contents, and executing a word search.

2. Update statutory research and locate research references using online statutory citators.

Instructions

1. An answer sheet is provided at the end of the questions for your convenience while you are working on the exercise. After you finish your research, submit your answers in typewritten form on a separate answer sheet. Do not retype the questions. Your answer sheet should contain only the answers to the questions.

2. If you spend more than 15 minutes trying to find the answer to any individual question, use the troubleshooting hints in the General Instructions for this Workbook. If you are still unable to find the answer, stop and seek assistance.

There are no separate problem sets for this exercise.

THE ASSIGNMENT

To answer the legal questions in this exercise, you will need to conduct statutory research using online resources. Answer the questions using only the text of the statutes you locate; do not conduct additional research.

You can locate statutes online in a variety of ways. Three common search techniques are: (1) retrieving a statute from its citation; (2) searching by subject using a statutory index or by browsing the table of contents of a code; and (3) executing a word search. Exercise 1.2, Introduction to Online Research, illustrates how to retrieve a statute from its citation. This exercise illustrates the subject and word searching options. You can also update statutory research and locate research references by using KeyCite in Westlaw or Shepard's in Lexis. You will use both updating services in the questions for this exercise.

I.   Review Questions

A.   How do federal public laws, session laws, and codified statutes differ?

B.   If you had a choice between using U.S.C. and U.S.C.S. (or U.S.C.A.) to research federal law, which would you use? Be sure to explain your answer.

C.   Explain the difference between an official code and an unofficial code.

II.   Westlaw

Begin your research by using Westlaw to locate authority relevant to the following research situation:

You are general counsel for a major medical center that is located in New Jersey. The medical center is a nonprofit entity (as defined under state and federal law) and relies on many volunteers to assist in providing comfort and assistance to patients and their families. Volunteers receive no compensation for their work and are not required to be licensed for the ministerial tasks they perform. Volunteers are instructed never to try to diagnose any ailment or provide any medication to any patient and to call for a member of the medical staff if any patient needs medical help.

Nick Whitehead was a volunteer at the medical center. He is trained as an actuary; he has no medical training of any kind. Mr. Whitehead was assisting a patient, Sonja Murillo, when Ms. Murillo complained of a headache. Instead of calling for a member of the medical staff, Mr. Whitehead provided Ms. Murillo with an over-the-counter headache medication that he carried for his personal use. Unfortunately, Ms. Murillo suffered serious complications from taking the over-the-counter medication because it was incompatible with several prescription medications she was taking. Ms. Murillo is now suing the medical center for negligence and Mr. Whitehead for gross negligence. You need to find out whether federal law protects the medical center or Mr. Whitehead from liability for Ms. Murillo's claims.

A.   Searching by Subject in Westlaw

One way to locate statutes is by searching by subject. Westlaw provides online access to the statutory index to many codes. Most online research services do not provide indices, but when one is available, it is an excellent way to search for statutes by subject. Browsing a code's table of contents is another way to search by subject and to make sure you locate all relevant provisions within a statute.

To determine whether federal law protects the medical center or a volunteer from negligence claims, begin by accessing the index to *United States Code Annotated,* the version of the federal code available in Westlaw. From the home page, choose the option to search United States Code Annotated (USCA). You can do this by following the link to "Statutes & Court Rules" under the "All Content" tab or by clicking on the "Federal Materials" tab. Once you access the USCA, look on the right margin for the list of "Tools & Resources." Click on the link to "United States Code Annotated Index" in the "Tools & Resources" list.

Once you have accessed the USCA statutes index, you will see an alphabetical list of index topics. Locate the index entry for "Volunteers" and subtopic "Protection." (Hint: Open the entry for Volunteers to see the subtopics listed under it.)

The index refers you to a section, followed by the notation "et seq." This means that the section referenced and following sections may be relevant to your research. Click on the link to the section referenced to view the section, and answer the questions below.

1. This is the first section of an act with multiple sections. Review the section you retrieved and the Historical and Statutory Notes under the History tab's Editor's and Revisor's Notes. What is the name of the section, and what is the short title of the act of which it is a part?

    (Hint: The short title appears in the Editor's and Revisor's Notes.)

2. Go back to the Document tab for this section. This section does not answer your research question. To view an outline of the rest of the sections in the act, click on the "Table of Contents" link. Provide the first and last section numbers of the act as listed in the table of contents.

3. Review the sections of the act, and answer the questions that follow:
    a. Is Mr. Whitehead a "volunteer" under the act? Provide the number of the section you used to answer this question. Be sure to explain your answer.
    b. Is Mr. Whitehead protected from liability for gross negligence under the act? Provide the number of the section you used to answer this question. Be sure to explain your answer.
    c. Is the medical center protected from liability for negligence under the act? Provide the number of the section you used to answer this question. Be sure to explain your answer.

B. Updating Statutory Research with KeyCite

Once you retrieve a section of a statute, you can use KeyCite to check it. The KeyCite entry will contain information on the history or status of the section, as well as the most complete listing of sources that have cited the section.

View the same section of the act you retrieved for the prior question (Question A1), and answer the questions below.

1. Review the annotations accompanying the statute. Are any cases summarized in the annotations? If so, how many? (Hint: Use the Notes of Decisions tab. Note that a case may be summarized more than once in the annotations. Be sure to count the total number of cases summarized (not the number of individual summary paragraphs) to answer this question.)

2. Although the Notes of Decisions can contain summaries of cases that cite a statute, not all are listed there. A citator will list all citing cases. To view cases citing the section, click on the "Citing References" link. How many citing cases appear in the KeyCite entry?

C.   Word Searching

In Westlaw, you can conduct a word search with or without selecting a database for your search. Because your search will retrieve many types of authority (statutes, cases, secondary sources, etc.), you can retrieve multiple forms of authority in a single search. If you are not sure what type of authority will help you answer a research question, or when you know you need multiple types of authority, a global search can be effective. But having all results in a single search may make it difficult to focus on the most relevant or most authoritative sources. You must evaluate the results carefully to make sure you locate and use the best authority available to resolve your research issue.

Continue your research into Ms. Murillo's claims by using a word search to determine whether state law applies to your research situation. Specifically, you need to determine whether state charitable immunity law protects the medical center from liability for Ms. Murillo's claim.

Locate the global search box. Use the jurisdiction selection box next to the search box to limit the jurisdiction to New Jersey. (Hint: Check the box for New Jersey and uncheck all other boxes.)

Enter the following search in the global search box, and execute the search:

charitable immunity

Review the search results. Notice that it retrieves thousands of documents organized by document type. Review the statutory results, and locate a statute that provides immunity from liability for negligence to nonprofit entities such as hospitals.

1. Provide the number of the section and the name of the annotated code.
2. Briefly describe what the section provides.
3. To claim charitable immunity, the medical center must qualify as a charitable institution. You need to find out whether this is a question for the court, or for the jury. The statutory language of the section you located for Questions 1 and 2, above, does not answer this question. Therefore, you must look for case law applying the statute to see if this question has been addressed.

    Review the Notes of Decisions accompanying the section. Is the determination of an entity's charitable status a question for the court or the jury? Provide the name and citation of a case that supports your answer. (Hint: The case summaries are organized by subject. Look for a subject heading that pertains to questions of law, or for the court. Click on the subject heading to go directly to case summaries under that heading.)

III.   Lexis

In this part of the exercise, you will continue your research by using Lexis to research Florida state statutes to answer the following research question:

A patient received an organ transplant at a branch of the medical center located in Florida. The patient required a blood transfusion during the procedure. Although the transplant was successful, the patient developed a rare form of hepatitis from the blood transfusion and is seriously ill. Instead of bringing a tort claim, the patient has filed a breach of contract claim against the medical center. The patient alleges that the provision of blood constituted a contract for the sale of goods and that the medical center's use of tainted blood violated an implied warranty in the contract. You need to research Florida state law to determine whether any statutory provisions address the exclusion or modification of implied warranties to blood provided for transfusions.

A.   Word Searching

For this part of the exercise, you need to research Florida state statutes. Use the drop-down menu on the right side of the red search box to limit the Jurisdiction to Florida and the Category to Statutes and Legislation.

Enter the search below:

blood and implied warranty

1. Review the search results. Provide the section number of the code section that seems most applicable to your research situation. (Hint: Identify a section in the Florida code, not a bill.)
2. Retrieve the section you listed in your answer to Question 1, above. Briefly summarize the relevant language from the statute.
3. Review the annotations accompanying the section. Scroll down until you find LexisNexis Notes and Case Notes. What must the plaintiff allege to maintain an action for breach of an implied warranty based on transfusion of tainted blood? Provide the name and citation of a case that supports your answer. (Hint: The case summaries are organized by subject. Look for a subject heading that pertains to blood and organ donations. Click on the blue downward arrow next to the subject heading to go directly to case summaries under that heading.)
4. The section you viewed is one section in a chapter comprised of multiple sections. To view an outline of sections in the chapter, scroll to the top of the document and click on the Table of Contents tab on the left side of the screen. Browse the table of contents to locate two additional sections in this chapter of the code, one that addresses the implied warranty of merchantability and one that addresses the implied warranty of fitness for a particular purpose. Provide the numbers of the sections in the annotated code.

B.   Shepardizing Statutes

You can check a statutory citation with Shepard's to locate information about the status of the statute and citations to sources that have cited the statute. Return to the statute you found for Question A1, above. Close the Table of Contents and click on the *"Shepardize* this document" link in the right margin.

Review the Shepard's entry, and provide the name and citation of a case decided by the Florida Supreme Court that cites the statute.

IV.   Bloomberg Law

In this part of the exercise, you will continue your research by using Bloomberg Law to research federal statutes to answer the following research question:

Additional blood tests on the patient who developed hepatitis revealed high levels of lead. The patient has lived for several years in an older home built in 1950 where lead-based paint might have been used. However, when the home was purchased the seller did not indicate lead-based paint was present. Is there a federal law that addresses lead-based paint in homes?

For this part of the exercise, you need to research federal statutes. From the Bloomberg Law home page, select Federal Law and then Federal Legislative. Select the United States Code (USC).

In the "Keywords" search box enter the search below:

lead-based paint

A.   Review the search results. Skim the Table of Contents Results to find the chapter dealing with Residential Lead-Based Paint Hazard Reduction. (Hint: Click "View More" to see the entire list.) Which chapter covers that topic?

B.   Open the chapter you listed in your answer to Question A., above. Review the sections within the subchapters to see which one addresses the disclosure of information concerning lead when residential property is transferred. (Hint: Click the gray plus-sign next to a subchapter to view the individual sections within that subchapter.) Cite the section of the United States Code that covers that disclosure.

C.   Review the statutory disclosure provision you found in Question B. A lead warning statement is required if a residential dwelling being transferred was built prior to what year? What are the five penalties for violating this section of the law?

D.   Open the Smart Code tab for the statutory section in Question C. How many cases have cited that section of the statute? Review the filtering options under the Smart Code Criteria for that section. From the Torts topic cases, provide the case name and citation of a 2015 case from the Eastern District of New York (E.D.N.Y.).

V.   Statutory Research on the Internet

The federal code and most state codes are available in unannotated form on the Internet. Depending on the source you use, you may be able to browse the code's table of contents, execute a key word search, or search for acts by popular name.

For this exercise, you are continuing your research into organ donation in your role as general counsel for a major medical center and must research the following situation:

The medical center's doctors have a patient (Patient A) who needs a kidney transplant. The patient's cousin (Donor A) is willing to donate a kidney but is not a biological match. The doctors' colleagues at a New York hospital have another patient (Patient B) who also needs a kidney transplant. Patient B's spouse (Donor B) is willing to donate a kidney but is not a biological match. As luck would have it, however, Donor B is a biological match to Patient A and could donate a kidney to Patient A, while Donor A is a biological match to Patient B and could donate a kidney to Patient B. The donors are willing to donate to their biological matches so that both patients can receive the transplants they need. The doctors know, however, that it is illegal to sell or trade organs for compensation, and they are not sure whether this proposed arrangement is legal. You need to locate state and federal law regarding organ sales to see whether this type of paired donation is permissible.

A.   State Statutory Research

For purposes of this exercise, assume that the procedures, if they are legal, would take place at the New York hospital, so you need to research New York law. You can locate New York statutes on the Internet in a variety of ways. One way is through Cornell Law School's Legal Information Institute website:

www.law.cornell.edu

From the home page, follow the links for "State law resources" and "Listing by jurisdiction." In the list of states, click on the link for New York, and choose the statutory option to search "New York Statutes," which takes you to the New York State Legislature site. Using the drop-down menu at the top of the page, select "Laws," and select "Laws of New York." This will bring up a search screen. You can execute a word search in the box above the listing of subjects covered in the consolidated laws. Execute the following search:

organ transplant

1.   Provide the subject name and section number of the provision that prohibits the sale of human organs.
2.   Review the section. Does it specifically authorize or prohibit the type of paired donation the medical center's doctors want to perform? Be sure to explain your answer.

B.   Federal Statutory Research

Having reviewed state law, you now need to research federal law to see if paired organ donation violates prohibitions on organ purchases. To research this issue, access the U.S. House of Representatives' website containing the United States Code:

http://uscode.house.gov

Choose the option to search the U.S. Code, and enter the following terms in the box for Search Word(s):

human organ donation purchase

1. Review the search results. Provide the title and section number of the U.S.C. that is most relevant to your research.

2. Is the type of paired donation the center's doctors would like to perform permissible under the statute? Be sure to explain your answer.

3. After the text of the statute, you will find historical notes about the statute, including notes about some amendments to the statute. Congress has amended the statute. How was the statute amended in 2007?

Exercise 6.1
Researching Statutory Provisions Online

Name: _____   Due Date: _____

Professor: _____   Section: _____

I.   Review Questions

A.

B.

C.

II.   Westlaw

A.   Searching by Subject in Westlaw

A.1.

A.2.

A.3.a.

A.3.b.

A.3.c.

B.   Updating Statutory Research with KeyCite

B.1.

B.2.

C.   Word Searching

C.1.

C.2.

C.3.

III.   Lexis

A.   Word Searching

A.1.

A.2.

A.3.

A.4.

B.   Shepardizing Statutes

Citation:

IV.   Bloomberg Law

A.

B.

C.

D.

V.   Statutory Research on the Internet

A.   State Statutory Research

A.1.

A.2.

B.   Federal Statutory Research

B.1.

B.2.

B.3.

Exercise 6.2
Researching with Statutory Indexes and Tables

Learning Outcomes

After completing this exercise, you should be able to

1. Locate statutes using the subject index and popular name table.

2. Locate research references using statutory annotations.

Instructions

1. An answer sheet is provided at the end of the questions for your convenience while you are working on the exercise. After you finish your research, submit your answers in typewritten form on a separate answer sheet. Do not retype the questions. Your answer sheet should contain only the answers to the questions.

2. If you spend more than 15 minutes trying to find the answer to any individual question, use the troubleshooting hints in the General Instructions for this Workbook. If you are still unable to find the answer, stop and seek assistance.

3. This exercise is tailored for online research, but you should also be able to complete the research with print resources. If you use print resources and are unable to find the answer to any individual question within 15 minutes, remember to refer to the troubleshooting hints in the General Instructions or seek assistance.

4. Although some questions include hints reminding you to update your research, others do not. Do not forget to update your research in all sources even if the question does not prompt you to do so.

5. If you conduct research in print, reshelve all books as soon as you finish using them.

Problem Sets

A B C D E F G H I J K L M N O

THE ASSIGNMENT

You need to answer several legal questions by conducting statutory research. This exercise will guide you through the process of researching statutes using an index or table and locating information in statutory annotations. As you conduct your research, you will need to provide answers to the legal questions. Answer the legal questions for this exercise using only the text of the statutes you locate; do not conduct additional research.

I.   Annotated State Codes

A.   Starting Research with an Index

Locate the state code for your problem set to answer the questions below. If your professor does not require you to use a print code, access the version available on Westlaw.

State Code

Problem Set A	*Arizona Revised Statutes Annotated*
Problem Set B	*West's Annotated California Codes*
Problem Set C	*West's Colorado Revised Statutes Annotated*
Problem Set D	*Connecticut General Statutes Annotated*
Problem Set E	*West's Florida Statutes Annotated*
Problem Set F	*West's Smith-Hurd Illinois Compiled Statutes Annotated*
Problem Set G	*West's Indiana Statutes Annotated*
Problem Set H	*Iowa Code Annotated*
Problem Set I	*West's Annotated Code of Maryland* or *Michie's Annotated Code of Maryland*
Problem Set J	*Vernon's Annotated Missouri Statutes*
Problem Set K	*McKinney's Consolidated New York Laws Annotated*
Problem Set L	*Purdon's Pennsylvania Consolidated Statutes Annotated*
Problem Set M	*West's Annotated Code of Virginia*
Problem Set N	*West's Revised Code of Washington Annotated*
Problem Set O	*Jurisdiction assigned by your professor; or Michigan Compiled Laws Annotated if unassigned*

A note about state codes: For Problem Sets A through N, this exercise directs you to use a specific version of a state's code. A state's code may be published by more than one publisher. If you use a version of the state code different from the one specified above, you should be able to locate the correct statutory provisions, but the index entries and information in the annotations may differ between the two versions of the code.

Often the answer to a question involving statutory research will not be found in a single section of the code. Instead, statutory research ordinarily requires you to research the complete statutory scheme, which may encompass multiple sections of the code. Many statutory schemes include a definitions section defining key terms, which can help you determine whether the scheme applies to the issue you are researching. To answer the state statutory research question in this exercise, you will need to locate the definitions section of a statutory scheme.

Here is your research situation:

You are general counsel for a major medical center and are responsible for ensuring that the center's policies and procedures comply with state law. The medical center wants to expand its services to include removing and transplanting human tendons through its orthopedic center. A tendon is not an organ; it is classified as human tissue. You know that state law regarding anatomical gifts applies to donations of body parts such as organs. You need to find out whether human tendons constitute body parts under the anatomical gift law.

1. Locate the general index for the state code. From the Westlaw home page you will want to find the "Statutes & Court Rules" for your assigned jurisdiction. You can do this by going to "State Materials" and clicking on your state or by going to "All Content," clicking on "Statutes & Court Rules," and then the state. Once you reach the page with the state's statutes you will see the index under "Tools & Resources" at the right margin. The index will refer you to relevant statutory provisions on the subject you are researching. For your research situation, look up the following search terms:

Anatomical Gifts
Definitions
OR
Anatomical Gifts
Generally

    (Hint for Problem Set L: The index entry for Anatomical Gifts refers you to the entry for "Gifts." Look up the term "Gifts," and then locate the subheading for "Anatomical Gifts.")

    The index may refer you to a specific section containing definitions, or it may refer you to a range of sections. The designation "et seq." refers to sections following the one listed in the index entry. If the index refers you to multiple sections, you will need to review the referenced sections to locate the definitions section.

    (Hint for Problem Set O: You may need to review different or additional subject entries in the index to find the information you need.)

    Go to the section(s) listed in the index, and locate the section containing definitions. If using the print code be sure to check the pocket part and soft cover supplement, if any. If the section has been enacted recently, it may not appear in the main volume of the code and may appear only in the pocket part or soft cover supplement.

    Provide the subject name, if appropriate, and section number for the section containing definitions. If you were given the option of using print or Westlaw, indicate which one you used. (Hint: Some state codes are organized by subject names, e.g., "Education § 100." If the code for your problem set is organized by subject, provide the subject name along with the section number for the section containing definitions. If not, provide only the section number.)

2. Define the term "body part," "part," or "body." Be sure to check the pocket part and soft cover supplement, if any, to update your research if you are using a print code. (Hint: The precise term that appears in the definitions section will vary depending on which problem set you complete.)

3. Review the annotations to the definitions section. The annotations list sources that have cited or discussed the code section, as well as other research references. Provide the information requested about the source listed for your problem set. On Westlaw, the tabs across the top provide access to that information. The tab for Context & Analysis, for example, includes references to law review articles and encyclopedias.

(Hints for print research: If the statute appears in the main volume, be sure to check the pocket part or soft cover supplement for updated annotations. If the statute appears in both the main volume and pocket part, the annotation source could be in either place.)

Annotation Information

Problem Set A	Arizona	The name and citation of a 2007 law review article
Problem Set B	California	The name and citation of a 1993 law review article
Problem Set C	Colorado	The citation of a practice aid concerning anatomical gifts made by a donor (Regarding His or Her Own Organs)
Problem Set D	Connecticut	The citation of a practice aid concerning definitions and procedural requirements
Problem Set E	Florida	The name and citation of a 1970 law review article by Luis Kutner
Problem Set F	Illinois	The name and citation of a 1983 case
Problem Set G	Indiana	The name and citation of a 1996 case
Problem Set H	Iowa	The name and citation of a 2008 law review article
Problem Set I	Maryland	The language inserted in, or added to, subsection (d) by amendment in 2008
Problem Set J	Missouri	The name and citation of a 1996 law review article
Problem Set K	New York	The name and citation of a 1975 case
Problem Set L	Pennsylvania	The name and citation of a 2003 law review article
Problem Set M	Virginia	The name and citation of a 2000 law review article
Problem Set N	Washington	The name and citation of a 2008 case
Problem Set O	Michigan if no jurisdiction is assigned	The name of a source listed in the annotations. If no sources are listed, answer "none" for this question. For Michigan, give the name and citation of a 1996 case.

4. Based on the information you found, does human tissue constitute a body part under state law governing anatomical gifts? Be sure to explain your answer.

B.   Using a Statutory Outline

As noted above, statutory research ordinarily requires you to research a complete statutory scheme. You will need to locate an additional section of the statute you located for Question A, above, to complete your research into the following matter:

In addition to determining the applicability of state anatomical gifts laws to tendon transplant procedures, you also need to evaluate the medical center's procedures for organ donations. The existing policy places no restrictions on which physicians may participate in an organ donation procedure. You are concerned that this policy may need to be revised to comply with state law.

Often, a code will provide an outline of the sections in a particular chapter or title. A good way to find related code provisions (including the provision you need to answer the questions below) is to use the statutory outline that appears at or near the beginning of the article, subchapter, chapter, or title of the code. (Hint: On Westlaw look for the "Table of Contents" or the hot-linked headings at the top of the statute. In a print set the outline usually appears in the main volume of the code. If the statute has recently been enacted or substantially modified, you may find a full or partial outline in the pocket part or soft cover supplement.)

1. Locate the section of the act addressing which physicians may participate in an organ donation procedure. This information appears in a provision that relates to procurement organizations, and more specifically, addresses rights and/or duties of an organ procurement organization upon the donor's death.

    (Hint: for Problem Sets E and K: Locate the section involving rights and duties at death.)

    (Hint for Problem Set F: Review the table of contents for the entire act, including Article 5.)

    (Hint for Problem Set L: Review the table of contents for the entire act, and locate the section involving rights and duties at death.)

    (Hint for Problem Set N: Locate the section concerning physical removal of donated body parts.)

    Provide the section number. Which physicians, if any, are prohibited from participating in procedures to remove or transplant a donated organ?

2. Based on what you found, does the medical center need to revise its policy? If not, why not? If so, how does the policy need to be changed?

II.   Federal Codes

The process of federal statutory research is similar to the process for state statutory research. To answer the questions below, locate one of the following sources:

United States Code Annotated (U.S.C.A.) in print or Westlaw
United States Code Service (U.S.C.S.) in print or Lexis
United States Code (U.S.C.) in Bloomberg Law

You can research the federal code using a subject index. The subject index will refer you to titles and sections within the federal code that pertain to the subject you are researching. Sometimes Congress names an act. These acts, such as the USA Patriot Act, are known by their popular names. If you know the popular name of an act, you can find its citation in the Popular Name Table in U.S.C.A. or the Table of Statutes by Popular Name in U.S.C.S. These tables list statutes alphabetically by name and will direct you to the title(s) and section(s) where the act is codified.

For this part of the exercise, you are continuing your research into matters affecting the medical center. You need to research the federal code to answer the questions for your problem set. Using *either* the subject index *or* the popular name table for *either* U.S.C.A. *or* U.S.C.S., locate statutory provisions that answer the federal statutory question for your problem set.

If you are conducting research with Westlaw: Follow the link to "Statute & Court Rules" under the "All Content" tab or click on the "Federal Materials" tab to access the USCA. Once you access the USCA, look on the right margin for the list of "Tools & Resources" to find the United States Code Annotated Index and United States Code Annotated Popular Name Table.

If you are conducting research with Lexis or Bloomberg Law: Lexis and Bloomberg Law do not include a statutory index, so you should use the popular names table.

In Lexis, under "Explore Content" choose "Statutes and Legislation," "Federal," and then "Codes" to see the USCS Popular Name Table.

In Bloomberg Law, select "Federal Law," then "Federal Legislative," and then "United States Code (USC)." Scroll to the bottom of the table of contents and place the cursor over "United States Code (USC) Popular Name Table" to access the search function.

Federal Statutory Question

Problem Set A, B, C, D, & E	You are continuing your review of the medical center's policies and procedures. The medical center offers ophthalmic services and operates its own optometry office. The individuals who work in the optometry office are licensed by the state to prescribe corrective lenses and dispense glasses and contact lenses. You need to find out whether the optometry office is subject to the Fairness to Contact Lens Consumers Act. Specifically: (1) Are the individuals who dispense contact lenses through the optometry office considered contact lens "prescribers"? (2) Under what circumstances are contact lens "prescribers" required to provide a patient with a written copy of the patient's contact lens prescription? (Hint: If you search a popular name table online, use the name of the act in quotation marks as your search to locate the entry for the act within the table.)

Problem Set F, G, H, I, & J	The medical center treats patients from across the country, and many patients must travel long distances for treatment. The medical center runs a nonprofit foundation that provides housing for patients' family members if those family members live a long distance from the medical center. The foundation wants to begin a fundraising campaign by placing calls to people across the U.S. to solicit funds for the family housing program. You need to find out whether this fundraising effort is subject to the Telemarketing and Consumer Fraud and Abuse Prevention Act. Specifically: (1) Would a telephone campaign seeking charitable contributions from people across the country constitute "telemarketing"? (2) If the foundation were to violate federal telemarketing rules, how long would a private person have to bring a civil action against the foundation? (Hint: If you search a popular name table online, use the name of the act in quotation marks as your search to locate the entry for the act within the table.)
Problem Set K, L, M, N, & O	The medical center treats many children. It operates a website for children facing serious illnesses. The website collects personal information from children and therefore is subject to federal law governing children's online privacy. You need to review the policies and procedures for operation of the website to make sure they comply with the Children's Online Privacy Protection Act of 1998. Specifically: (1) Does the law governing online privacy apply to a "child" age 13? (2) Can the medical center, as the operator of the website, be held liable under state or federal law for disclosing a child's personal information to the child's parent? (Hint: If you search a popular name table online, use the name of the act in quotation marks as your search to locate the entry for the act within the table.)

A. Indicate how you located the relevant act.

B. The act spans multiple sections of the code. Provide the number of the title where the statute is codified, and provide the section numbers for the first and last sections of the statute. (Hint: You may need to retrieve the first section of the act and view the code's table of contents to find this information.)

C. Review the chapter outline, and locate the provisions that answer the federal statutory questions for your problem set.

   1. Briefly answer the first question. Provide the section number of the section where you found the answer. Be sure to explain your answer.

   2. Briefly answer the second question. Provide the section number of the section where you found the answer. Be sure to explain your answer.

Exercise 6.2
Researching with Statutory Indexes and Tables

Name: _____   Due Date: _____

Professor: _____   Section: _____

Problem Set: _____

I.   Annotated State Codes

A.   Starting Research with an Index

A.1.

A.2.

A.3.

A.4.

B.   Using a Statutory Outline

B.1.

B.2.

II.   Federal Codes

A.

B.

C.

C.1.

C.2.

Exercise 6.3
Researching Statutes on Your Own

Learning Outcomes

After completing this exercise, you should be able to

1. Locate statutes to answer a legal question.

2. Update statutory research.

Instructions

1. An answer sheet is provided at the end of the questions for your convenience while you are working on the exercise. After you finish your research, submit your answers in typewritten form on a separate answer sheet. Do not retype the questions. Your answer sheet should contain only the answers to the questions.

2. If you spend more than 20 minutes researching the legal question, use the troubleshooting hints in the General Instructions for this Workbook. If you are still unable to find the answer, stop and seek assistance.

3. This exercise is tailored for online research, but you should also be able to complete the research with print resources. If you use print resources and are unable to find the answer within 20 minutes, remember to refer to the troubleshooting hints in the General Instructions or seek assistance.

4. Do not forget to update your research even though the questions do not prompt you to do so.

5. If you conduct research in print, reshelve all books as soon as you finish using them.

Problem Sets

A   B   C   D   E   F   G   H   I   J   K   L   M   N   O

THE ASSIGNMENT

The medical center for which you conducted statutory research in Exercises 6.1 and 6.2 has come back to you with additional legal questions, set out below. Using the code for the jurisdiction for your problem set, conduct statutory research to determine the answers to the questions. The facts provided with the questions should lead you to a statutory scheme relevant to the questions. Unless your professor instructs you differently, answer the questions using only the text of the code section(s) you locate; do not conduct additional research.

If your professor permits you to choose between print and online research for this exercise, you may want to conduct research both ways to compare your results.

Here is the research situation:

A shortage of doctors in some rural areas makes it difficult for some patients to receive timely care. The medical center hopes to bridge that gap using telemedicine. Health care professionals in the medical center would interact with patients via the web. However, the medical center wants to see if there are any legal impediments to starting such a program and what requirements must be met in your jurisdiction. (Hint: For questions concerning "telemedicine" or "telehealth," using those terms in the code's online or print index may be a good starting point.)

Problem Set	Jurisdiction	Legal Questions
A	Arizona	1. What is the definition of telemedicine under Arizona's public health and safety laws? 2. What does Arizona law require a health care provider to obtain before health care can be delivered to a patient through telemedicine?
B	California	1. What is the definition of telehealth under the California Business & Professions Code section covering enforcement of the rules of medicine for physicians and surgeons? 2. Does the use of telehealth in the section of the California law you found in question 1 include "telemedicine" as used in the Code of Federal Regulations (C.F.R.)?
C	Colorado	1. What is the definition of telehealth under Colorado's insurance provisions governing health care coverage as of Jan. 1, 2017? 2. Does use of telephone or email fall within the definition of telehealth (as of Jan. 1, 2017)?
D	Connecticut	1. What is the definition of telehealth under Connecticut's public health and well-being laws? 2. Does that law permit a facility fee to be charged for services delivered via telehealth?
E	Florida	1. Under Florida law governing a license or permit for an internet pharmacy, what is the minimum number of hours each week that patients must have access to a pharmacist via a toll-free telephone line? 2. What are the requirements for someone to be a prescription department manager and receive an internet pharmacy permit?
F	Illinois	1. What is the definition of telemedicine under Illinois laws regulating health professions and occupations? (Hint: Locate the definition of telemedicine, not telehealth.) 2. What issue did the legislature want to address with the law?

G	Indiana	1. What is the definition of telemedicine under Indiana's health insurance laws? 2. Does the use of a telephone constitute a telemedicine service?
H	Iowa	1. Under Iowa law permitting pharmacy sales via the internet, is it possible for a pharmacy to limit liability? Explain your answer. 2. Is an internet pharmacy required to disclose its physical location? If so, how must it be done?
I	Maryland	1. What is the definition of telemedicine services under Maryland's health insurance laws? 2. Does the law permit patients in rural and urban locations to be treated differently?
J	Missouri	1. What is the purpose of using telehealth technology in the Volunteer Health Services Act's ECHO program? 2. What is the full name of the ECHO program and who manages it?
K	New York	1. What is the definition of telehealth under New York's public health laws generally (and not specific to health maintenance organizations)? 2. Does the law provide a separate definition for telemedicine? If so, give it.
L	Pennsylvania	1. What is the definition of telemedicine under Pennsylvania's Patient-Centered Medical Home Advisory Council Act? 2. How was telemedicine expected to assist the advisory council in its duties to develop an organizational model?
M	Virginia	1. What is the definition of telemedicine services under Virginia laws governing health insurance coverage? 2. Are Virginia insurers required to provide coverage for telemedicine services?
N	Washington	1. What is the definition of telemedicine under Washington's laws governing home health care? 2. Does the law provide for reimbursement for the cost of purchasing or leasing telemedicine equipment?
O	Jurisdiction assigned by your professor; or Michigan	1. What is the definition of telemedicine under the state's health insurance laws? 2. Who can provide telemedicine services?

I.　Conducting Research

Record all the steps in your research process.

II.　Determining Which Statute Applies

List the statutory provision(s) you located.

III.　Answering the Legal Questions

Answer the legal questions using the code section(s) you located. Be sure to explain your answers.

Exercise 6.3
Researching Statutes on Your Own

Name: _____   Due Date: _____

Professor: _____   Section: _____

Problem Set: _____

I.   Conducting Research

Steps:

II.   Determining Which Statute Applies

Statutory provision(s):

1.

2.

III.   Answering the Legal Questions

Answer:

1.

2.

Chapter 7

FEDERAL LEGISLATIVE HISTORY RESEARCH

Exercise 7.1
Researching the Legislative History of a Federal Statute Using Statutory Annotations

Learning Outcome

After completing this exercise, you should be able to locate documents in the legislative history of a specific federal statute by statutory annotation in Westlaw.

Instructions

1. An answer sheet is provided at the end of the questions for your convenience while you are working on the exercise. After you finish your research, you must submit your answers in type-written form. Do not retype the questions. The answer sheet should contain only the answers to the questions.

2. If you spend more than 15 minutes trying to find the answer to any individual question, use the troubleshooting hints in the General Instructions for this Workbook. If you are still unable to find the answer, stop and seek assistance.

Problem Sets

A B C D E

For letters F to O use the top letter above yours in the chart below unless directed otherwise. For example, letter M does problem set **C**.

A	B	C	D	E
F	G	H	I	J
K	L	M	N	O

THE ASSIGNMENT

You can research federal legislative history in two ways: You can search for the history of a specific statute, or you can search legislative history by subject. This exercise covers research into the legislative history of a specific statute, which is the way lawyers most frequently conduct legislative history research. Exercise 7.2 covers research into legislative history by subject.

For this exercise, you need to conduct research on legislative history related to your Client Matter, below. Although secondary sources, related statutes, and cases interpreting the statute can help you understand the statute, you have decided that you need to research the statute's legislative history to understand fully how the statute applies to your client's situation.

While you can conduct legislative history research in print, this exercise requires you to use only online sources.

I.   Review Questions

A.   List four sources of federal legislative history.

B.   Rank the four sources you listed for Question A, above, in order from most authoritative to least authoritative, with source number 1 being the most authoritative and source number 4 being the least authoritative.

C.   Briefly explain why the source you ranked first in Question B, above, is considered the most authoritative source of legislative history.

II.   Using Statutory Annotations to Research the Legislative History of a Specific Statute

To research the legislative history of a specific federal statute, you first need to locate the statute and review the legislative information provided with the statute. U.S.C.A. annotations in Westlaw contain references to the statute's Public Law (Pub. L.) number and its *United States Statutes at Large* (Stat.) citation, which are useful in researching legislative history. The annotations' "History" tab includes selected committee reports, *Congressional Record* entries, and other documents concerning the legislation. Annotations in Lexis and Bloomberg Law include references to the Public Law number and *United States Statutes at Large,* but not to committee reports. (Lexis and Bloomberg Law include recent and selected historical committee reports. In Lexis you can look under "Federal Legislative Bill History." In Bloomberg, go to Federal Law>Federal Legislation>U.S. Congress.)

Review the Client Matter. Use the search box in Westlaw to retrieve the provision in U.S.C.A. for your problem set.

Client Matter and Statutory Provision

Problem Set A	You work for an organization that promotes leave policies for workers who wish to take time off work in order to have a child, raise a child, or care for a sick or ailing family member. You seek to research federal law providing for such leave.	29 U.S.C.A. § 2612
Problem Set B	You work for an organization that advocates for the rights of individuals with disabilities. You seek to research federal law prohibiting employment discrimination against persons with disabilities.	42 U.S.C.A. § 12112
Problem Set C	You work for an organization that promotes free and fair elections in the United States. You wish to research federal law establishing standards for voting systems.	52 U.S.C.A. § 21081
Problem Set D	You work for an organization that advocates against human trafficking. You seek information on federal programs to combat human trafficking.	~~42 U.S.C.A. § 14044c~~ 34 U.S.C.A. § 20705
Problem Set E	You work for an organization that advocates for easier voter registration and voting procedures. You wish to research federal requirements for voter registration.	52 U.S.C.A. § 20504

A. Briefly, in a sentence or two, describe what the section provides.

B. The Public Law number and *United States Statutes at Large* citation for the section as originally enacted and for any subsequent amendments appear in parentheses immediately after the text of the statute and before the annotations.

   Review the parenthetical following the text of the section you located for Question A, above, to answer the following questions.

   1. Provide the Public Law number and *United States Statutes at Large* citation for the section as it was originally passed (not for any subsequent amendments).

      (Hint: Look for the earliest Public Law number and *United States Statutes at Large* citation.)

   2. Click on the Public Law number link of the original Public Law to bring up the text of the original Act. (Hint: Click on the earliest linkable Public Law number.) What is the name of the Act?

   3. Now go back to the statute. Has the statute been amended by later acts of Congress? If so, how many times has it been amended?

C. Access the committee report for your problem set. Locate the link to the committee report under the "History" tab. The report you need may appear in the "Legislative History Materials" section, the "Editor's and Revisor's Notes" section, or both.

Click on the link to the report, and answer the following questions.

Committee Report Citation

Problem Set A	Senate Report No. 103-3, January 27, 1993
Problem Set B	House Report No. 101-485(II), May 15, 1990
Problem Set C	House Conference Report No. 107-730, October 8, 2002
Problem Set D	House Report No. 109-317(I), November 18, 2005
Problem Set E	House Report No. 103-9, February 2, 1993

1. Provide the name of the committee that issued the report you located.

2. Before the statute was passed into law, it was assigned bill numbers in both the House of Representatives and the Senate. Provide the bill number for the version of the bill considered by the congressional committee that issued the report you located. (Hint: Look for the "S" number for bills considered by a Senate committee, and look for the "H.R." number for bills considered by a House committee.)

3. Provide the date of the Act's consideration in the Senate. If more than one date is listed, provide the latest date. (Hint: Be sure to provide the latest date, not the earliest (first) date.)

4. Skim the document, and answer the committee report question for your problem set below. (Hint: Go past the full text of the bill if it is reproduced at the beginning of the report to answer the question.)

Committee Report Question

Problem Set A	According to the section on Background and Need for Legislation, what problems does this legislation address?
Problem Set B	According to the section on Summary of the Legislation, what is the purpose of the ADA?
Problem Set C	According to the first paragraph of the report, what is the purpose of this legislation?
Problem Set D	According to the Purpose and Summary, what does the Act do?
Problem Set E	According to the Findings, what were some of the techniques developed to discourage participation in the late nineteenth and early twentieth centuries?

Exercise 7.1
Researching the Legislative History of a Federal Statute Using Statutory Annotations

Name: _____   Due Date: _____

Professor: _____   Section: _____

Problem Set: _____

I. Review Questions

A.

B.

C.

II. Using Statutory Annotations to Research the Legislative History of a Specific Statute

A.

B.1.

B.2.

B.3.

C.1.

C.2.

C.3.

C.4.

Exercise 7.2
Researching the Legislative History of a Federal Statute by Subject

Learning Outcome

After completing this exercise, you should be able to locate legislative history documents by subject in Lexis and in ProQuest Congressional or ProQuest Legislative Insight.

Instructions

1. An answer sheet is provided at the end of the questions for your convenience while you are working on the exercise. After you finish your research, you must submit your answers in type-written form. Do not retype the questions. The answer sheet should contain only the answers to the questions.

2. If you spend more than 15 minutes trying to find the answer to any individual question, use the troubleshooting hints in the General Instructions for this Workbook. If you are still unable to find the answer, stop and seek assistance.

Problem Sets

A   B   C   D   E

For letters F to O use the top letter above yours in the chart below unless directed otherwise. For example, letter M does problem set **C**.

A	B	C	D	E
F	G	H	I	J
K	L	M	N	O

THE ASSIGNMENT

In addition to locating legislative history through statutory annotations, as in Exercise 7.1, you can also locate legislative history by subject using a word search. This exercise requires you to use Lexis to search the *Congressional Record* for floor debates and a subscription service, ProQuest Congressional or ProQuest Legislative Insight, for committee testimony. Although this exercise requires you to use these specific services, you can also use Westlaw, Bloomberg Law, or government resources such as Congress.gov to locate selected floor debates in the *Congressional Record*, and you can use Westlaw or Bloomberg Law to locate selected committee testimony.

I.   Locating Legislative History in the *Congressional Record*

This section requires you to locate a floor debate in the *Congressional Record* using Lexis.

To locate the *Congressional Record* database in Lexis, under "Explore Content" click on "Statutes and Legislation" for content type, then click on "Congressional Record." (Do not select older subsets of dates.) *Congressional Record* should appear to the right of the search box as a filter.

Enter the search phrase below in the search box and execute the search to find the document indicated below for your problem set. (Hints: Be sure to type the search terms exactly as they appear below, including the quotations, and sort by relevance.)

Congressional Record Search

Problem Set A	Search Phrase: "Family and Medical Leave Act of 1993"
	Document: House debate, beginning at 139 Cong. Rec. H396
Problem Set B	Search Phrase: "Americans with Disabilities Act"
	Document: House debate, beginning at 136 Cong. Rec. H2599
Problem Set C	Search Phrase: "Help America Vote Act"
	Document: House debate, beginning at 147 Cong. Rec. H9264
Problem Set D	Search Phrase: "Trafficking Victims Protection Reauthorization Act"
	Document: Senate debate, beginning at 151 Cong. Rec. S14417
Problem Set E	Search Phrase: "National Voter Registration Act of 1993"
	Document: House debate, beginning at 139 Cong. Rec. H505

Locate the link for "Table of Contents" that corresponds to your document in the vertical box on the left side of the screen. Clicking that box opens a link to "View full table of contents," which takes you to your designated page within the Table of Contents for the entire *Congressional Record*. (This allows you to see where your debate occurs in relationship to other congressional actions on this day, and beyond.) Click the link, and look for the Cong. Rec. citation in blue.

A.   Based on the Table of Contents entry alone, what action occurred, or what bill was considered, immediately before the debate on your bill? (Hint: Look for the entry in all caps on the line above the entry for the debate on your bill.)

Now go back to your search results. Click on the link to the *Congressional Record* indicated for your problem set. Skim the floor debate, and answer the *Congressional Record* questions, below, for your problem set. (Hint: Sometimes the full text of the bill under consideration will be reproduced in the *Congressional Record*. Scroll down past the text of the bill to find the answer to the question.)

Congressional Record Questions

Problem Set A	1. According to Representative Reed, in which state is this legislation already the law?	2. According to Representative Reed, in a word, does the legislation work in this state?
Problem Set B	1. According to Representative Hoyer, what has the ADA been designed to do?	2. Briefly, according to Representative Hoyer, what do the last remaining amendments deal with?
Problem Set C	1. According to Representative Nye's summary of the bill's purposes, why does the bill's program provide funds to the States?	2. According to Representative Nye's introductory remarks, what new Commission assists in the administration of Federal elections and provides assistance with the administration of certain Federal election laws and programs?
Problem Set D	1. According to Senator Leahy, what does this reauthorization confirm?	2. According to Senator Leahy, how has the reauthorization package been significantly improved?
Problem Set E	1. According to Representative Swift, what is the rather unfortunate tradition in this country that the Act is designed to eradicate?	2. According to Representative Swift, what does the legislation do for those in economic distress?

B.   Answer the first *Congressional Record* question for your problem set.

C.   Answer the second *Congressional Record* question for your problem set.

II.   Locating Legislative History in Committee Testimony

This section requires you to locate committee testimony using ProQuest Congressional or ProQuest Legislative Insight. Locate the home page for ProQuest Congressional or ProQuest Legislative Insight on your library's portal. (Hint: ProQuest Congressional and ProQuest Legislative Insight are subscription services. Therefore, you may need a password or code to access these services from a computer outside the library.)

Click on the "Advanced Search" link under "Congressional Publications" (which may be "Legislative & Executive Branch Publications" in some libraries) or the "Guided Search" link. Change the pull-down menu to "All fields *including* full text," and search only for "Hearings." (Hint: Uncheck the boxes for Publication Type, and check only "Hearings.")

Enter the search phrase below in the first search box. Execute the search, and locate the document indicated for your problem set. (Hint: Use the Narrow filters to limit your results by date.)

Search Phrase and Document

Problem Set A	Search Phrase: "Bankruptcy Abuse Prevention and Consumer Protection Act of 2001"
	Document: Hearing on "Bankruptcy Abuse Prevention and Consumer Protection Act of 2001," February 7-8, 2001
Problem Set B	Search Phrase: "Sports Agent Responsibility and Trust Act"
	Document: Hearing on "Sports Agent Responsibility and Trust Act," May 15, 2003
Problem Set C	Search Phrase: "Animal Fighting Prohibition Enforcement Act"
	Document: Hearing on the "Animal Fighting Prohibition Enforcement Act of 2005," May 18, 2006
Problem Set D	Search Phrase: "Fair Pay Restoration Act"
	Document: Hearing on "Fair Pay Restoration Act: Ensuring Reasonable Rules in Pay Discrimination Cases," January 24, 2008
Problem Set E	Search Phrase: "health care reform"
	Document: Hearing on "America's Need for Health Reform," September 18, 2008

If you are using **ProQuest Congressional**:

For Question A, use the Contents page of the hearing to go to the Testimony to review the list of witnesses.

For Question B, select "Retrieve selected transcripts" and review the testimony of the indicated witness.

If you are using **ProQuest Legislative Insight**:

Click on the "PDF" link to pull up the full committee report.

For Question A, use the Table of Contents near the beginning of the report to review the list of witnesses.

For Question B, turn to the corresponding page in the report, and review the testimony of the indicated witness. (Hint: You can use the witness's actual statement or his or her prepared remarks to answer this question.)

Committee Testimony Questions

| Problem Set A | A. What is the name and position of the U.S. Chamber of Commerce official who testified on February 7, 2001? | B. According to the official, what is the "primary factor," or a "substantial factor," driving the rise in bankruptcies? |

Problem Set B	A. What is the name of the subcommittee that held the hearing on H.R. 361, the Sports Agent Responsibility and Trust Act, on May 15, 2003?	B. According to Chairman Chris Cannon, what is the result of the multi-million dollar value of professional athletes' salaries, signing bonuses, and endorsement contracts?
Problem Set C	A. What is the name and position of the law enforcement officer who testified on May 18, 2006?	B. According to the officer, what peripheral criminal activity is associated with dog fighting?
Problem Set D	A. What is the name and school of the law professor who testified on January 24, 2008?	B. The law professor makes three essential points about the *Ledbetter* decision. Briefly, what is the law professor's first point?
Problem Set E	A. What is the name of the Governor of the State of New Jersey, who testified on September 18, 2008?	B. According to the Governor, what is a severe problem for our state economies, one that impacts our ability to work in healthcare?

A.   Answer the first Committee Testimony Question for your problem set.

B.   Answer the second Committee Testimony Question for your problem set.

Exercise 7.2
Researching the Legislative History of a Federal Statute by Subject

Name: _____   Due Date: _____

Professor: _____   Section: _____

Problem Set: _____

I. Locating Legislative History in the *Congressional Record*

A.

B.

C.

II. Locating Legislative History in Committee Testimony

A.

B.

Exercise 7.3
Researching the Legislative History of a Federal Statute with Congress.gov

Learning Outcome

After completing this exercise, you should be able to locate documents in the legislative history of a specific federal statute online using Congress.gov, the Library of Congress website.

Instructions

1. After each question, you will find space to write your answer. This is for your convenience while you are working on the exercise. After you finish your research, you must submit your answers in typewritten form. Do not retype the questions. The answer sheet should contain only the answers to the questions.

2. If you spend more than 15 minutes trying to find the answer to any individual question, use the troubleshooting hints in the General Instructions for this Workbook. If you are still unable to find the answer, stop and seek assistance.

There are no separate problem sets for this exercise.

THE ASSIGNMENT

With online research tools, you can research the history of an individual federal statute, or you can search by subject. This exercise requires you to use Congress.gov, a public website maintained by the Library of Congress, to research the legislative history of a specific federal statute.

Congress.gov contains a wealth of legislative information. Some of its databases contain historical documents dating back many years, while others contain information only since about 1995. Therefore, you need to assess Congress.gov's coverage to see if it contains the information you need. You can also use Congress.gov to trace the progress of pending bills as they make their way through the legislative process.

Using Congress.gov, you can search in a variety of ways, including by bill number, Public Law number, committee, or subject. You can also conduct word searches in Congress.gov's databases.

Use Congress.gov to research the following matter:

You work for an organization that researches and advocates for good public health policies. You know that Congress passed, and the President signed, landmark legislation in 2009 and 2010 that would impose certain requirements to expand health insurance coverage to most Americans. You wish to research the legislative history of this Act.

Go to Congress.gov and answer the questions below.

I.   Click on the "Legislation" link at the top of the page. Enter the following search phrase in the search box and select "All Legislation" on the left:

affordable care act

In the search results, find H.R. 3590 in the 111th Congress (2009-2010), the "Patient Protection and Affordable Care Act." Click on the link for "H.R. 3590," and answer the following questions.

A.   Open the Overview box near the top of the page, if it is not already open. According to the Overview, who is the sponsor of this Bill?

B.   Which Committee in the House of Representatives reported this Bill?

II. Now click the "Text" tab to see the Public Law version of the Bill.

A.   Review the table of contents (near the top of the results screen), and locate Section 1001 of the Bill. What is the title of Section 1001?

B.   Section 1001 of the Bill amends several sections of the Public Health Service Act. Locate the amendment to Section 2714, "Extension of dependent coverage," in the table of contents. Now scroll past the table of contents to review the text of the amendment to Section 2714. What does subsection (a) provide?

III. Now click the "Actions" tab, and click the "Actions Overview" button on the left-hand side of the page.

A.   Locate the entry for "Passed/agreed to in Senate." Click on the "Record Vote Number: 396" link. How did Senator Sanders (I-VT) vote on the Bill?

B.   Go back to the "Actions" page. On what date did the President sign the Bill?

IV. Click the "Amendments" tab.

A.   How many total amendments were offered to this Bill?

B.   Click on the link to Senate Amendment 3298, "S. Amdt. 3298." Very briefly, what is the purpose of this amendment?

C.   Review the "Overview" box. What was the Latest Action on this amendment?

V.   Go back to the main page for the Bill. Click on the link for "Related Bills." Locate S. 2964, "Strengthening Program Integrity and Accountability in Health Care Act." Click on the link for "S.2964."

A.   Click on the "Text" tab. Briefly, according to the introductory language, what is the purpose of this legislation?

B.   Click on the "Actions" tab. What was the last action on this legislation?

Exercise 7.3
Researching the Legislative History of a Federal Statute
with Congress.gov

Name: _____   Due Date: _____

Professor: _____   Section: _____

I.A.

I.B.

II.A.

II.B.

III.A.

III.B.

IV.A.

IV.B.

IV.C.

V.A.

V.B.

Chapter 8

FEDERAL ADMINISTRATIVE LAW RESEARCH

Exercise 8.1
Researching Federal Administrative Regulations from a Statute

Learning Outcomes

After completing this exercise, you should be able to

1. Locate and interpret regulations in the *Code of Federal Regulations* (C.F.R.).

2. Locate and interpret regulatory history in the *Federal Register*.

Instructions

1. An answer sheet is provided at the end of the questions for your convenience while you are working on the exercise. After you finish your research, submit your answers in typewritten form on a separate answer sheet. Do not retype the questions. Your answer sheet should contain only the answers to the questions.

2. If you spend more than 15 minutes trying to find the answer to any individual question, use the troubleshooting hints in the General Instructions for this Workbook. If you are still unable to find the answer, stop and seek assistance.

There are no separate problem sets for this exercise.

THE ASSIGNMENT

A client has come to you with a client matter, set out below. The client matter is an issue addressed by a federal statute and implementing regulations published in the *Code of Federal Regulations* (C.F.R.) and the *Federal Register*. You have decided that you need to research the implementing regulations to understand completely how the statute applies to your client's situation. This exercise will guide you through the process of researching federal regulations.

You can complete the exercise using print resources, Westlaw, or Lexis. Some questions can also be answered using Bloomberg Law, HeinOnline, or websites maintained by the federal government.

I.   Review Questions

A.   How often, and on what schedule, is the C.F.R. published?

B.   One way to locate regulations in the C.F.R. is through cross-references to the C.F.R. in U.S.C.A. and U.S.C.S. Briefly describe a second way to locate regulations in the C.F.R.

C.   Are regulations in the C.F.R. binding or nonbinding authority on an issue within an agency's jurisdiction? Be sure to explain your answer.

II.   Researching Federal Regulations Using Statutory Annotations

One way to locate federal regulations is through the annotations following the enabling statute in U.S.C.S. and U.S.C.A. Your client has come to you with the following matter, which requires regulatory research:

Your client, Authentic Reenactment, would like to import and sell three types of imitation guns: (1) Realistic-looking, non-firing replicas of guns used during the Civil War for use in Civil War battle reenactments; (2) realistic-looking, non-firing guns used during World War I for use in World War I battle reenactments; and (3) small decorative versions of both types of guns for sale as souvenirs. The federal government requires imitation guns to contain markings indicating that they are not real firearms. You need to find out if the federal requirements apply to the products your client wants to import.

A.   The federal statute that applies to your client's products is 15 U.S.C. § 5001, Penalties for entering into commerce of imitation firearms. Locate this section of the federal code in U.S.C.A. (in print or in Westlaw) or U.S.C.S. (in print or in Lexis), and answer the questions below.

1.   Read the statute, including the acts prohibited under the statute and the statutory definitions. Would it be unlawful for your client to import either Civil War or World War I replica guns that do not contain the required markings? Be sure to explain your answer.

2.   Review the portion of the statute that describes the required markings. The statute defines the required markings but then grants authority to the Secretary of Commerce to alter those requirements. What authority does the Secretary of Commerce have with respect to look-alike guns used in theatrical productions?

3.   The Secretary of Commerce has adopted regulations published in the C.F.R. implementing the requirements of the statute. Review the statutory annotations and find the cross-reference to the regulations. Provide the citation to the portion of the C.F.R. that contains the regulations. The relevant portion may be identified by Title and section number followed by the notation "et seq.", or it may be identified by Title and Part. Both types of references indicate that relevant

regulations appear in multiple sections of the C.F.R. (Hints for locating cross-references to the *Code of Federal Regulations*: In Westlaw, look under the "Context and Analysis" tab. In Lexis, scroll to the bottom of the page, to "Research References & Practice Aids.")

4. Look up the section or Part you identified for Question A3, above, in the C.F.R. in print or by clicking on the appropriate link. (Hint: If the relevant portion was identified by Part, locate the first section in the Part.) Read the regulation. The marking requirements do not apply to decorative objects that meet certain size requirements. What are those size requirements?

5. The C.F.R. includes references to the *Federal Register* (FR) volume and page where the regulation was published before it was codified in the C.F.R. In print, the reference may appear in brackets immediately following the regulation or at the beginning of the Part, directly after the table of contents. In Westlaw and Lexis, *Federal Register* references follow the text of the section.

   a. Locate the citation to the *Federal Register* notice published on January 23, 2013, that refers to the regulation you located. Provide the citation, as it appears in the C.F.R., to the *Federal Register* volume and page number. (Hint: The *Federal Register* is abbreviated "FR" in the C.F.R. and in Lexis and Westlaw. "Fed. Reg." is the abbreviation often used in citations.)

   b. Review that same section of the C.F.R. and find the citation to an earlier version of the regulation published in the *Federal Register* on October 26, 1992. Give the citation to the *Federal Register* as it appears in the C.F.R.

B. Just as statutory research often requires you to research a statutory scheme, federal administrative law research often requires you to research a regulatory scheme. To do this, you will need to review the table of contents for the C.F.R. Part containing regulations relevant to your client matter.

   In Westlaw or Lexis: From the regulation you read for Question A4, above, click on the "Table of Contents" link to view the table of contents. (Hint: You may need to scroll up or down to view the entire table of contents for the Part.)

   In print: From the regulation you read for Question A4, above, turn back to the beginning of the C.F.R. Part to locate the table of contents for the Part.

   (C.F.R. citations can also be retrieved from Bloomberg Law and govinfo.gov.)

1. Using the table of contents, locate the C.F.R. sections that address approved markings and waivers from the marking requirements. Provide the title and section numbers.

2. Review the C.F.R. section that addresses approved markings. Pursuant to the statute, the regulations provide that one way an imitation gun may be identified is with an orange plug inserted into the barrel. The statute also permits the Secretary to specify other ways that imitation guns may be marked. List three *additional* ways (other than an orange plug) that an imitation gun may be identified.

3. Review the C.F.R. section that addresses waivers. What argument can you make to support your client's request for a waiver?

III.   Researching Regulatory History in the Federal Register

Having researched your client's question using the C.F.R., you decide that you would like to learn more about the regulatory history of an applicable C.F.R. section. The *Federal Register* prints regulations, proposed regulations, and a brief description of the regulatory history of codified regulations.

The *Federal Register* entry for your regulation begins with the name of the implementing agency. Many, though not all, *Federal Register* entries also contain sections titled "Summary," "Effective Date," "Further Information," and "Supplemental Information" with information on the regulatory history of the section. The final regulations, as they appear in the C.F.R., appear only after these sections.

To learn more about the regulation you located in Part IIA, above, locate the *Federal Register* entry you located in Question IIA5(b), above, from October 26, 1992. (Hint: You may notice that the regulations' section numbers are different in the *Federal Register* notice than they are in the C.F.R. This is because these regulations were renumbered in 2013.)

In Westlaw or Lexis: Click on the link to the *Federal Register* (FR) citation following the text of the regulation or enter the citation to retrieve the document. Depending on which service you use, this may take you to the beginning of the entry, or it may link directly to the first reference to the regulation within the entry. You may need to navigate back a page or two to the beginning of the entry to find the portions of the entry describing the changes to the regulation to answer the question below. (Hint: Be sure to use the link or citation to the *Federal Register* for October 26, 1992 that appears after the section you located for Part IIA, above, concerning the size requirements; links following other sections may not retrieve the correct information.)

In print: Locate the *Federal Register* set in your library. To locate the issue you need, use the *Federal Register* Date chart. The citation refers directly to the page where the amended regulation appears. You will need to review earlier portions of the entry describing the changes to the regulation to answer the question below.

(*Federal Register* notices are also available in Bloomberg Law and some government websites.)

Review the "Background" section of the entry. (Hint: You may have to scroll up or down to find it.)

Why did the regulations establish an alternative marking system (other than an orange plug inserted into the barrel of the gun) for certain kinds of imitation guns?

Exercise 8.1
Researching Federal Administrative Regulations from a Statute

Name: _____   Due Date: _____

Professor: _____   Section: _____

Problem Set: _____

I.   Review Questions

A.

B.

C.

II.   Researching Federal Regulations Using Statutory Annotations

A.1.

A.2.

A.3.

A.4.

A.5.a.

A.5.b.

B.1.

B.2.

B.3.

III.   Researching Regulatory History in the *Federal Register*

Exercise 8.2
Researching Federal Administrative Regulations Using Government Websites

Learning Outcomes

After completing this exercise, you should be able to locate federal administrative materials in the *Code of Federal Regulations* (C.F.R.) and *Federal Register* using the Federal Government's govinfo.gov and agency websites.

Instructions

1. An answer sheet is provided at the end of the questions for your convenience while you are working on the exercise. After you finish your research, submit your answers in typewritten form on a separate answer sheet. Do not retype the questions. Your answer sheet should contain only the answers to the questions.

2. If you spend more than 15 minutes trying to find the answer to any individual question, use the troubleshooting hints in the General Instructions for this Workbook. If you are still unable to find the answer, stop and seek assistance.

There are no separate problem sets for this exercise.

THE ASSIGNMENT

This exercise requires you to use government websites to locate federal administrative materials. For this exercise, you will use online sources to research legal issues raised by your client, Newton Financial Services.

I. Researching Federal Regulations Using an Agency Website

The federal government makes much administrative material available free of charge via the Internet. Like federal legislative history, federal administrative law research is easily accomplished using government websites. Some government websites, such as the Federal Government's govinfo.gov site, contain the full text of the C.F.R. Others, such as agency websites, limit their coverage to laws, regulations, and other materials in the subject area the agency regulates. If you practice regularly in an area of law regulated by a federal agency, you will become familiar with the agency sites and the unique types of information they contain. A list of agency websites is at www.usa.gov.

Use the federal government websites listed below to research the following question raised by your client:

Your client, Newton Financial Services, is a brokerage corporation subject to a number of federal laws, including the Occupational Safety and Health (OSH) Act and the Consumer Financial Protection Act of 2010. Consequently, it must comply with Occupational Safety and Health Administration (OSHA) standards and regulations. Newton Financial Services received a citation from an OSHA inspector for several violations of the OSH Act. Newton Financial Services has asked you whether it must notify employees of the citation. You need to research OSHA citations to find out what your client's obligations are with respect to notifying employees.

A. First you need to find the provisions of the OSH Act of 1970. You know that OSHA provides access to occupational safety laws and regulations, so you decide to begin with the agency's website. Go to www.osha.gov to locate the information you need.

   There are several ways to locate the act. Use the "Law & Regulations" drop-down menu on the OSHA homepage, and then select "OSHA Law and Regulations." You can also locate the act by using the search box to search for the OSH Act of 1970 or by searching through the A-Z Index.

   1. Click on the link for the OSH Act. (Hint: If you navigate from the drop-down menu, you may need to scroll down the page to find a link to the OSH Act.) Review the table of contents for the OSH Act and locate the section regarding citations. Provide the section number.

   2. Click on the link to the section. The section describes the process for issuing citations. Where must an employer post a citation?

   3. In the version of the Act on the OSHA website, the sections are numbered as they appear in the Public Law enacted by Congress. The OSH Act is also codified within U.S.C. The codified citation appears in the right margin. Provide the citation to the section on citations as it appears in U.S.C.

B. Because the statute gives the Secretary of Commerce authority to issue regulations regarding posting citations, you must research regulations to see if Newton Laboratories must fulfill any additional requirements in posting the citation. You can locate regulations on the OSHA website in several ways. You may use the "Law & Regulations" drop-down menu. You can also look up "Regulations & Laws" or "Standards" in the A-Z Index. (Hint: Be sure to choose the option to view "All.")

   Locate the link to Title 29 of the C.F.R., Part 1903, addressing Inspections, Citations, and Proposed Penalties. Click on the link to bring up an outline of C.F.R. sections within Part 1903. Locate the regulation that addresses posting citations.

   1. Provide the number of the section (also called a "Standard") you located.

   2. Review the section. For how long must Newton Financial Services post the citation?

II. Researching Federal Regulations Using General Government Research Websites

A. Although an agency website is a convenient source for administrative information, it is not an official source for the regulations. The Government Printing Office (GPO) is the official online source for federal regulations. GPO is transitioning the site of official regulations from the Federal

Digital System (FDSys) to a new site, govinfo.gov. To continue your research in an official database, access official regulations at:

govinfo.gov

One reason Newton Financial Services received a citation was because it failed to post required information about the OSH Act where employees could see it. Newton Financial Services wants to correct this violation by posting a copy of a poster approved by the state's Department of Labor and has asked you how large the poster must be to comply with OSH regulations. Using the search functions on govinfo.gov, look up 29 C.F.R. § 1903.2, concerning requirements for informing employees about OSH Act protections. (Hint: You should be able to retrieve the regulation from its citation using the "Most Recent" version of the C.F.R.)

1. What is the title of this section?
2. Review the regulation. What are the size and type requirements for the poster?

B. The official source for all federal regulations is the C.F.R. GPO provides online access to official regulations. Unlike commercial sources such as Lexis and Westlaw, the official print and online versions of the C.F.R. are not continuously updated to include changes published in the *Federal Register*. However, GPO does provide online access to C.F.R. Parts Affected as recently as the past 24 hours. (This information is presently available at www.fdsys.gov but will transition to govinfo. gov.)

The government also has a version of the C.F.R. that is continuously updated: the Electronic CFR (e-CFR). The e-CFR is a version of the C.F.R. that is updated daily to incorporate changes to regulations published in the *Federal Register*. You can use the e-CFR to update research from an official version of the C.F.R. To answer the questions below, access the e-CFR at:

www.ecfr.gov

1. Read the "User Notice" at the beginning of the e-CFR. Although the e-CFR is updated daily, it is not a source you should cite for a regulation. Why?
2. Newton Financial Services has been informed that a former employee has filed a complaint with OSHA alleging that the company retaliated against her for reporting violations of the Consumer Financial Protection Act of 2010. Browse the e-CFR to locate 29 C.F.R. Part 1985, which contains regulations governing retaliation complaints. Identify the "Source" of the regulations at the beginning of the part. Provide the *Federal Register* citation and date.
3. Now go back to govinfo.gov. Use the citation you found for Question 2, above, to retrieve the *Federal Register* entry for the final rule. Were any changes made to the final rule based on comments submitted regarding the interim rules? Why or why not? (Hint: Search for the phrase *public comment* within the document to locate discussion of comments submitted.)

Exercise 8.2
Researching Federal Administrative Regulations
Using Government Websites

Name: _____   Due Date: _____

Professor: _____   Section: _____

I.   Researching Federal Regulations Using an Agency Website

A.1.

A.2.

A.3.

B.1.

B.2.

II.   Researching Federal Regulations Using General Government Research Websites

A.1.

A.2.

B.1.

B.2.

B.3.

Exercise 8.3
Researching Federal Administrative Regulations on Your Own

Learning Outcome

After completing this exercise, you should be able to locate and interpret regulations in the *Code of Federal Regulations* (C.F.R.).

Instructions

1. An answer sheet is provided at the end of the questions for your convenience while you are working on the exercise. After you finish your research, submit your answers in typewritten form on a separate answer sheet. Do not retype the questions. Your answer sheet should contain only the answers to the questions.

2. If you spend more than 20 minutes researching the legal question, use the troubleshooting hints in the General Instructions for this Workbook. If you are still unable to find the answer, stop and seek assistance.

3. Do not forget to update your research even though the questions do not prompt you to do so.

4. If you conduct research in print, reshelve all books as soon as you finish using them.

There are no separate problem sets for this exercise.

THE ASSIGNMENT

Your client has approached you with the client matter below. The client matter is an issue that can be answered by reference to federal regulations. You need to research federal regulations relevant to the client matter.

You can complete the exercise using print resources, government websites, Westlaw, Lexis, or Bloomberg Law.

Client Matter

Your client wants to begin manufacturing children's bicycle helmets and has asked you for guidance regarding the Consumer Product Safety Commission's safety standards for bicycle helmets. Specifically, you need to find out how many sample helmets your client must test for compliance with safety standards, which specific tests it must conduct, and what instructions must appear on the helmet labels.

I.   Locating Federal Regulations

A.   Locate regulations that resolve the client matter, and provide the title and section numbers for the regulations.

B.   Explain how you located the regulations.

II.   Resolving the Client Matter

Based on the results of your research, answer your client's questions:

A.   How many sample helmets must your client test for compliance with safety standards?

B.   Which four safety tests must your client conduct?

C.   What instructions must appear on the helmet labels?

Exercise 8.3
Researching Federal Administrative Regulations on Your Own

I.   Locating Federal Regulations

    A.

    B.

II.   Resolving the Client Matter

    A.

    B.

    C.

Chapter 9
ONLINE SEARCH TECHNIQUES

Exercise 9.1
Online Search Techniques

Learning Outcomes

After completing this exercise, you should be able to

1. Explain how differences in database coverage affect search results.

2. Explain how to limit and refine search results.

3. Demonstrate appropriate use of Boolean search techniques in Westlaw, Lexis, and Bloomberg Law.

Instructions

1. An answer sheet is provided at the end of the questions for your convenience while you are working on the exercise. After you finish your research, you must submit your answers in type-written form. Do not retype the questions. The answer sheet should contain only the answers to the questions.

2. If you spend more than five minutes trying to find the answer to any individual question, use the troubleshooting hints in the General Instructions for this Workbook. If you are still unable to find the answer, stop and seek assistance.

There are no separate problem sets for this exercise.

THE ASSIGNMENT

The purpose of this exercise is to illustrate how online search results differ depending on the scope of the database you select and the Boolean (terms and connectors) search options you use.

To illustrate the effects of the search options, some of the searches in this exercise will retrieve very large numbers of documents, while others will retrieve very few. Remember, however, that a search is neither effective nor ineffective based solely on the number of documents it retrieves. If many authorities are relevant to your research, you want to retrieve all the relevant documents. If few authorities are relevant, you want to be able to target those few authorities. The purpose of this exercise is simply to show you how various search options will affect your search results. In each research project you do, you will have to decide which approaches are most likely to retrieve the information you need.

The first step in online searching is selecting an online service in which to search. For this exercise, you will use Westlaw, Lexis, and Bloomberg Law. The questions that follow direct you to execute a variety of searches.

I.   Westlaw

A.   Selecting a Database or Jurisdiction

If you decide to research in Westlaw, you may select a database in which to execute a search. The database you select defines the content through which Westlaw will look for your search terms. The scope of your research project will determine the appropriate database(s) in which to search.

In Westlaw you can designate a database (including a jurisdiction) for your search by selecting from the "Browse" box. You can also designate a jurisdiction in the jurisdiction box next to the universal search box. Finally, you can designate a jurisdiction *after* you execute your search by using the "Narrow" filters on the left side of the search results screen.

For the questions below, assume that you need to research state case law concerning crimes associated with illegal drug use among students at school.

1.   Select the jurisdiction for "All States." (Hint: Be sure to de-select any federal jurisdiction.) Execute this search:

> student and school and drug and illegal

How many cases does the search retrieve?

2.   Now change the jurisdiction to "California," and execute the same search. How many documents does this search retrieve?

If you were researching the law of all 50 states, "All States" might be an appropriate jurisdiction for your search. If you were researching only California state law, however, "California" would be a better choice, because it would limit the search results to authority from California state courts.

3.   Assume that you decided to change the scope of your search to include cases from the California state courts and federal cases from the Ninth Circuit. From the jurisdiction menu, select "California" and "9th Circuit." Execute the same search as above. How many cases does the search retrieve? (Note that this search will also automatically retrieve relevant U.S. Supreme Court cases and federal district court cases within the Ninth Circuit.)

4. Now assume that you want to search only California state cases, cases from the United States Court of Appeals for the Ninth Circuit, and all federal district court cases from California. Click the View for Cases on the left side of the search results screen. Use the "Narrow" filters to designate your jurisdictions to include all California state cases, all Ninth Circuit cases, and all cases from the federal district courts in California. (Hint: Be sure to select all the federal district courts in California.) How many cases does the search retrieve?

B.   Constructing and Executing a Search—Boolean Search Techniques

After you select a database, the next steps are constructing and executing a search. Westlaw allows you to search with or without Boolean search commands. Effective use of Boolean search commands can improve your search results. The following questions illustrate the use of connectors and search phrases.

1.   Connectors

The connectors you use to connect search terms can greatly affect the search results.

For questions a and b, below, assume that you need to continue your research into crimes associated with illegal drug use among students at school. Now, however, you are researching all federal law.

a. From the jurisdiction menu, select "All Federal." (Hint: Be sure to uncheck California in the jurisdiction menu.) Type this phrase into the search box, and execute the search:

student and school and drug and illegal

How many cases does the search retrieve?

b. Now change the connectors from "and" to "/p" (meaning "within the same paragraph"). (Hint: You can also use the "Advanced Search" option and type this phrase into the box designated for "All of these terms.") Execute this search:

student /p school /p drug /p illegal

How many cases does the revised search retrieve?

The more restrictive the connectors, the fewer documents the search retrieves. The broader the connectors, the more documents the search retrieves. "And" is the broadest connector.

2.   Search phrases

Another way to alter your search results is to group terms together in search phrases.

The notion of a bona fide residence may arise in cases involving qualifications for municipal employment, voting, taxing, licensing, and other areas. Assume that you are researching bona fide residences in Illinois and want to research Illinois cases.

a. Designate "Illinois" as your jurisdiction. (Hint: Be sure to uncheck All Federal in the jurisdiction menu.) Type this phrase into the search box and execute the search:

bona fide residence

How many cases does the search retrieve?

b. Click on "Advanced" next to the search box to access the "Advanced Search" page. Type that same phrase into the box designated for "This exact phrase," and execute the search. How many documents does the revised search retrieve?

To search for a particular phrase in Westlaw, use the Advanced Search box designated for "This exact phrase." Do not use the boxes designated for "Any of these terms" or "All of these terms" because the results will include irrelevant cases.

C.   Limiting and Refining Search Results

You can limit and refine your search by using the "Document Fields" in the Advanced search option or the "Narrow" filters on the left side of the case results screen.

1. A "document field" is an individual component of a document, such as its citation or title. When you use a field restriction, the search is run only within the specified component of the document.

    Assume you need to research federal court cases within the Seventh Circuit in which the State of Illinois is a party. Designate "7th Circuit" in the jurisdiction box next to the search box. (Hint: Be sure to uncheck Illinois in the jurisdiction menu.)

    Click on "Advanced" next to the search box to access the "Advanced Search" page. Delete the search terms from the prior search. Type "Illinois" into the "Name/Title" box under "Document Fields." Execute the search. How many cases does the search retrieve?

Note that this search retrieves every case in which the term "Illinois" appears in the case name. Although this will retrieve decisions in which the State of Illinois is a party, it retrieves many other decisions, too.

2. Now refine your search to find cases involving quid pro quo (literally "this for that") in employment discrimination. Click on "Advanced" to gain access to the advanced search options. Type "quid pro quo" into the box designated for "This exact phrase." (Hint: Be sure that "Illinois" still appears in the "Name/Title" box.) Execute the search. How many cases does the revised search retrieve?

3. Refine your search further by using the "Narrow" filters on the left side of the search results screen. (Hint: Be sure to designate "Cases" as your "View.") Select the United States Court of Appeals for the Seventh Circuit as your Jurisdiction, and select the topic "Employment & Labor." How many cases does your revised search retrieve?

4. Click on the "View" for "Secondary Sources." Provide the title and citation of a law review article from 1995 that has "sexual harassment" in the title. (Hint: Filter by "Law Reviews & Journals" and date.)

Note that you may narrow your case search using other filtering criteria, including date, reported status, judge, attorney, law firm, Key Number, party, and docket number. These options appear under "Narrow" on the left side of the search results screen.

II.   Lexis

A.   Selecting a Database or Jurisdiction

Just as you can select a database or jurisdiction for your search in Westlaw, you can select a database or jurisdiction for your search in Lexis. You can select a database or jurisdiction using the drop-down menu to the right of the red search box. The "Explore Content" box also allows you make those selections. You can also select a database or jurisdiction using the browse options above the red search box. Finally, you can select a database or jurisdiction *after* you execute your search by using the "Narrow By" options on the left side of the search results.

Assume that you are researching adverse possession.

1. Using the drop-down menu to the right of the red search box, limit your initial search to the United States Supreme Court. Enter the following search in the red search box:

adverse possession

Execute the search, and click on the "Cases" sub-tab. How many cases does this search retrieve?

2. Now change the jurisdiction filter to "Virginia" and execute the new search. (Hint: Be sure to remove the United States Supreme Court filter.) How many cases does this new search retrieve?

3. Assume that you wish to research only Virginia Supreme Court cases. Using the "Narrow By" options on the left side of the search results screen, find the "Court" options. Click on the link for the Virginia Supreme Court. How many cases does this new search retrieve?

4. Assume that you decide to expand the scope of your search to include federal cases. In the drop-down menu next to the search box, modify the jurisdiction by checking the box to "Include related Federal content." Execute the new search. How many cases does this new search retrieve?

5. To find related secondary sources, click the sub-tab "Secondary Materials." Provide the title and citation of a 2012 law review article from the *Virginia Journal of Social Policy and the Law.*

B.   Constructing and Executing a Search—Boolean Search Techniques

Like Westlaw, Lexis allows you to search with or without Boolean search commands.

1.   Connectors

Just as you can use connectors in Westlaw to refine your search, you can use connectors in Lexis to refine your search.

a.   Clear the search box. (Hint: Be sure that your jurisdiction is set to "Virginia" and "related Federal content.") Type this phrase into the search box, and execute the search:

adverse /s possession

How many cases does the search retrieve?

b.   Now replace the "/s" with "/2" so that the new search phrase reads as follows:

adverse /2 possession

How many cases does this search retrieve?

The connector "/s" tells Lexis to search for any document in which the word "adverse" appears in the same sentence as the word "possession." As a result, your search results may include documents that have nothing to do with adverse possession (because the words are used in an entirely different context, even if in the same sentence). In contrast, the connector "/2" tells Lexis to search for any document in which the word "adverse" appears within two words of the word "possession." These results are more likely to include documents that use the phrase "adverse possession."

Lexis allows you to use other connectors to refine your search. These are displayed by selecting "Advanced Search."

2.   Search Phrases

In Lexis you can also refine your search using Boolean commands by selecting "Advanced Search."

a.   Return to the home page. Set your jurisdiction to "Virginia" and "Include related Federal content." Click on "Advanced Search." Type the phrase below in the "This exact phrase" box and click "Add." (Note that the phrase appears in quotation marks in the red search box.)

adverse possession

Execute the search. How many cases does the search retrieve?

b.   Now assume that you wish to eliminate results that involve adverse possession of housing. Under "Narrow By" in the left margin find the "Search Within Results" box. Enter the following search phrase in that box:

not hous!

Execute the search. How many cases does the search retrieve?

The extender "!" tells Lexis to search for any word that starts with "hous," including "house," "houses," and "housing." Lexis has other extenders, which are listed under "Use Connectors" in the "Advanced Search" tab. Note that this search may eliminate more results than you wish, because a document may use the words "house," "houses," or "housing" even if the document does not involve adverse possession of housing. The same results can be achieved by entering this search in the top search box: "adverse possession" and not hous!

C.   Limiting and Refining Search Results

You can limit and refine your search results in Lexis using the content category, jurisdiction, and practice-area menus in the "Explore Content" box, "Browse" drop-down, and red search box drop-down filters. You can also use the "Narrow By" options on the left side of the search results screen.

1. From the home page under "Explore Content" select "Briefs, Pleadings and Motions." Click on "Federal Briefs" and then "U.S. Supreme Court Briefs." Enter the following search phrase in the red search box:

    "adverse possession" and not hous!

    Provide the name of any United States Supreme Court case from 2007 in which a party filed a brief using the phrase "adverse possession," but not the words "house," "houses," or "housing" (as required by your search parameters).

2. Use the drop-down filter in the search box and check "Virginia" and "Include related Federal content." (Lexis will ask you to confirm that you want to replace the existing filter for U.S. Sup. Ct. Briefs; click "Continue.") Using the same search phrase from C.1, above, execute the search. After selecting "Cases" on the left side of the search results screen, use the "Narrow By" options below that and go to "Timeline." Designate dates from January 1, 2000, to December 31, 2010, and click "OK." How many cases does this search retrieve?

III.   Bloomberg Law

A.   Selecting a Database or Jurisdiction

Just as you can select a database or jurisdiction for your search in Westlaw and Lexis, you can select a database or jurisdiction for your search in Bloomberg Law. From the "Getting Started" box you can drill down to the database you want to search. You also can choose one of the tabs across the top, such as "Search & Browse," to select a database. Finally, you can select a database or jurisdiction *after* you execute your search in the <GO> bar by using the "Filter Your Results" options on the left side of the search results screen.

For the questions below, assume that you need to research state case law concerning comparative negligence.

1. Select "Illinois" as your jurisdiction. (Hint: Select "All Legal Content" and drill down to U.S. Courts, Court Opinions, State Court Opinions. Click on "Illinois" to make that your database.) Enter this phrase in quotes in the "Keywords" search box:

    "comparative negligence"

    How many cases does this search retrieve?

2. Now assume you only want to look at Illinois Supreme Court cases on the issue. Look under "Filter Your Results" on the left and check the box for Illinois Supreme Court. How many cases are given?

3. Assume that you want to see if there are any cases from the United States Court of Appeals for the Seventh Circuit on the issue. Change the jurisdiction to "Seventh Circuit Court of Appeals," and run the same search. (Hint: Drill down to U.S. Courts, Court Opinions, Federal Court Opinions, U.S. Court of Appeals, and then click on Seventh Circuit Court of Appeals. Be sure that Illinois is no longer selected. You can click a red circled "x" to remove the source.) How many cases does this search retrieve?

B.   Constructing and Executing a Search—Boolean Search Techniques

Like Westlaw and Lexis, Bloomberg Law allows you to search with or without Boolean search commands.

1.   Connectors

Just as you can use connectors in Westlaw and Lexis to refine your search, you can do so in Bloomberg Law.

a. Select "Illinois" as your jurisdiction. (Hint: Be sure to remove Seventh Circuit as a source.) Click open the "Search Help" under "Keywords" and click "More" to review the complete list of search operators. Which search proximity connectors enable you to retrieve results with search terms within the same sentence?

b. Type this phrase in the "Keywords" box and run the search:

    comparative /s negligence

    How many cases does the search retrieve?

c. Now assume that you also wish to find cases that mention "comparative fault" as well as "comparative negligence." Add the words "or fault" to your search phrase in the "Keywords" box so it reads:

    comparative /s negligence or fault

Execute the search. How many Illinois Supreme Court cases does the search retrieve?

2.   Search phrases

Another way to alter your search results is to group terms together in search phrases. To retrieve the exact phase in Bloomberg Law use quotation marks to surround the phrase.

Although some jurisdictions use the comparative negligence or comparative fault doctrine, others apply the contributory negligence doctrine. Assume that you are researching contributory negligence in Maryland and want to find cases that also mention "assumption of the risk."

a.   Select "Maryland" as your jurisdiction. Type the following into the "Keywords" search box and execute the search:

"contributory negligence" and "assumption of the risk"

How many cases does the search retrieve?

b.   After reviewing your search results it occurs to you that a court might have used the phrases "contributorily negligent" and "assumed the risk." Type the following into the Keyword search box and execute the search:

contributor! /2 negligen! and assum! /s risk

How many cases does the search retrieve?

The multiple character wildcard/expander "!" tells Bloomberg Law to search for any word that starts with the root given. For example, "assum!" retrieves "assume," "assumed," and "assumption." The "/2" connector requires that the words "contributor!" and "negligen!" be within two words of each other.

C.   Limiting and Refining Search Results

You can refine your search results in Bloomberg Law using the tools on the left side of the search results screen. From the "Search Criteria" box you can modify your search or restrict your results by date. In the "Filter Your Results" box you can limit case results by court, topic, or judge.

1.   Assume you now want to find federal district court cases from Maryland using the same search phrase from B.2.b, above. Select the "District of Maryland" as your jurisdiction. (Hint: Drill down to U.S. Courts, Court Opinions, Federal Court Opinions, U.S. District Courts, and then click on District of Maryland.) Execute the search. How many cases are given?

2.   Now assume you need to find a case involving products liability from those you have retrieved in C.1, above. Use "Filter Your Results" and check the box next to "Products Liability." Provide the name and citation to a case involving a truck rental company listed under the topic "Products Liability."

Exercise 9.1
Online Search Techniques

Name: _____   Due Date: _____

Professor: _____   Section: _____

I.   Westlaw

A.   Selecting a Database or Jurisdiction

A.1.

A.2.

A.3.

A.4.

B. Constructing and Executing a Search—Boolean Search Techniques

B.1.a.

B.1.b.

B.2.a.

B.2.b.

C. Limiting and Refining Search Results

C.1.

C.2.

C.3.

C.4.

II.   Lexis

A.   Selecting a Database or Jurisdiction

A.1.

A.2.

A.3.

A.4.

A.5.

B.   Constructing and Executing a Search—Boolean Search Techniques

B.1.a.

B.1.b.

B.2.a.

B.2.b.

C.   Limiting and Refining Search Results

C.1.

C.2.

III.   Bloomberg Law

A.   Selecting a Database or Jurisdiction

A.1.

A.2.

A.3.

B.   Constructing and Executing a Search—Boolean Search Techniques

B.1.a.

B.1.b.

B.1.c.

B.2.a.

B.2.b.

C.   Limiting and Refining Search Results

C.1.

C.2.

Chapter 10

RESEARCH PLANNING

Exercise 10.1
Developing and Executing a Research Plan

Learning Outcome

After completing this exercise, you should be able to develop and execute a comprehensive research plan to locate authority on a legal issue.

Instructions

1. An answer sheet is provided at the end of the questions for your convenience while you are working on the exercise. After you finish your research, you must submit your answers in typewritten form. Do not retype the questions. The answer sheet should contain only the answers to the questions.

2. If you conduct research using print sources, reshelve all books as soon as you finish using them.

Problem Sets
A   B   C   D   E

For letters F to O use the top letter above yours in the chart below unless directed otherwise. For example, letter M does problem set C.

A	B	C	D	E
F	G	H	I	J
K	L	M	N	O

THE ASSIGNMENT

Your client has come to you for advice about the legal questions set out in your problem set. To answer the legal questions, you will need to research the law using a variety of research tools. To complete this exercise, you will need to develop and execute a research plan. The questions in this exercise will guide you through the research planning process and help you locate authorities relevant to the legal questions. If appropriate for your problem set, your professor will assign a jurisdiction for your research.

Legal Questions

Problem Set A: State Common Law Research
Company v. Employee

Your client used to work as a salesperson for a company that provides IT and computer repair services to local individuals and businesses. The company provides services across three counties within your state, and your client's sales territory covered the entire service area. When your client began to work with the company, she signed an employment contract that contained a covenant not to compete. The covenant provides that your client cannot work in a sales position for a competitor that provides IT or computer repair services anywhere in the United States for a period of two years after leaving the company. The covenant states that the company believes this restriction is necessary to protect its business interests because salespeople have access to customer lists and other proprietary information.

Your client recently moved to another state 500 miles away to work for a competitor. The company sent a letter to your client threatening to sue her for violating the covenant not to compete unless she quits her new job. Your client has contacted you to find out whether the covenant is enforceable. What considerations or standards will a court use to evaluate the validity of the covenant not to compete?

Problem Set B: State Statutory Research
State v. Interceptor

You are a prosecutor who must decide whether to charge an individual with a crime based on the following facts: The director of Human Resources for a large corporation was faced with an urgent work matter, so she visited the president of the corporation at his home over the weekend to discuss the situation. The president was entertaining houseguests, so he and the Human Resources director went out to the back patio to talk. During the heated conversation, the Human Resources director made several unflattering comments about other members of the senior management team. Unbeknownst to either party to the conversation, a landscaper was working in the yard in an area concealed by bushes. The landscaper heard the conversation and recorded it using his cell phone. The recording contained no video images of the speakers, but their voices were clearly audible. The landscaper then provided the recording to local media outlets, which reported on management disagreements within the company. The landscaper may have violated state criminal statutes prohibiting unauthorized interception of certain types of communications. Research state criminal statutes, and analyze whether the conversation was the type of communication protected from interception by state statute.

(Hint: You may need to research cases interpreting the statute to answer the question.)

Problem Set C: Federal Statutory Research
United States v. Servicemember

Your client is a member of the armed forces. One evening she drank to excess while celebrating a friend's birthday. As the evening came to a close, one of your client's fellow servicemembers saw your client in an inebriated state and took her to task for drinking too much. Your client and the other servicemember had a history of disagreements, and your client did not react well to his comments. She referred to the other servicemember with a racial slur and said she would run him down with her car if she had the opportunity. The other servicemember became angry and told her to "pipe down." This enraged your client, who said, "I'm going to come after you right now." Before your client could take any action, her friends removed her from the situation. The next day she was charged under the federal Uniform Code of Military Justice (UCMJ) for her statements. You need to research whether her statements constitute provoking speech under the UCMJ.

(Hint: You will need to research cases interpreting the statute to answer the question.)

Problem Set D: State Procedural Research
Neighbor v. Neighbor

You are the clerk for a judge who must resolve a dispute between two neighbors over a tree. One of the neighbors wants to remove the tree. He believes he has obtained title from the other neighbor to the parcel of land where the tree is located through adverse possession, and therefore is entitled to remove the tree. He wants to remove it so he can erect a gazebo in his back yard in preparation for his daughter's wedding in two months. The other neighbor believes the tree is on property that she owns, and she opposes removal of the tree. The neighbor who opposes removal of the tree learned that the tree is scheduled to be removed tomorrow, so she filed a complaint in state court asking for a determination that the tree is on her property and also requesting a temporary restraining order to prevent removal of the tree. The judge has asked you to research temporary restraining orders. Research the procedural rule governing the issuance of a temporary restraining order and answer the following questions: (1) Under what circumstances may a temporary restraining order be issued without notice to the adverse party? (2) What is the maximum number of days a temporary restraining order can remain in effect before it expires (assuming it is not extended)?

(Hint: Use only the language of the rule, not cases interpreting the rule, to answer these questions.)

Problem Set E: Federal Procedural Research
Plaintiff v. Judge

You represent the plaintiff in a civil action filed in federal district court. The case was assigned to the Chief Judge of the district court. The judge refuses to issue a scheduling order or to take any action to allow the case to proceed. You have contacted the judge's chambers and filed motions requesting that the judge follow proper procedures so that the case can proceed to resolution either by motion or trial or be assigned to a different judge. All of your efforts have been ineffective. You have decided to investigate whether to petition the appellate court for a writ of mandamus to force the judge to take the necessary actions for the case to proceed. Research the Federal Rules of Appellate Procedure to answer the following questions: (1) What must a petition for a writ of mandamus state? (2) Is this the type of situation to which a writ of mandamus should be addressed?

(Hint: You will need to research cases interpreting the rule to answer the second question.)

I.   Obtaining Preliminary Information

List the preliminary information you know about the problem: due date, work product expected, limits on research tools to be used, jurisdiction, and whether nonbinding (or persuasive) authority should be located.

II.   Drafting a Preliminary Issue Statement

Prepare a preliminary issue statement.

III.   Generating Search Terms

List your search terms. Be sure to expand the breadth and depth of the list. (Hint: The charts in Exercise 2.1 can help you with this process.)

IV.   Planning and Executing Your Research Plan

A.   Search for binding (or mandatory) primary authority first. List the sources you plan to consult in the order you plan to consult them. For each source, indicate whether you will conduct your research in print or online and why you chose print or online research. (Hint: Remember that even in a search for binding primary authority, secondary sources can often be a good starting point because they provide background information and citations to primary authority.)

B.   Begin your research, keeping notes as you work. Indicate below the order in which you actually consulted each source. If the order differed from your original plan, explain why. In addition, list any online searches you executed.

C.   List up to three binding primary authorities you plan to use to analyze the legal questions you are researching. Briefly explain how you located each authority and why you plan to use it.

D.   Remember to update each authority you plan to use. List the steps you took to update each authority.

E.   Assess your research results. Do you need to locate nonbinding authority (nonbinding primary authority or secondary authority) to complete your analysis? Why or why not?

F.   If you do not need to locate nonbinding authority, skip to Question J, below.

   If you do need to locate nonbinding authority, plan your research for locating this additional authority. List the sources you plan to consult in the order you plan to consult them. For each source, indicate whether you will conduct your research in print or online and why you chose print or online research. (Hint: Remember that secondary sources can be effective for locating nonbinding primary authority.)

G.   After planning your research path for locating nonbinding authority, continue your research, keeping notes as you work. Indicate below the order in which you actually consulted each source. If the order differed from your original plan, explain why. In addition, list any online searches you executed.

H.   List up to three nonbinding authorities (primary or secondary) you plan to use to analyze the legal questions you are researching. Briefly explain how you located each authority and why you plan to use it.

I.   Remember to update each nonbinding authority you plan to use. List the steps you took to update each authority.

J.   Assess your research results. Has your research come full circle, in that the authorities you have located have begun to refer back to each other and the new authorities you locate fail to reveal significant new information?

K.   If the answer to Question J, above, is yes, skip to Part V, below, because your research is complete. If your answer to Question J is no, explain the further steps you plan to take to complete your research.

V.   Answering the Legal Questions

Once you have completed your research, you are ready to draft answers to your client's legal questions. Write a brief analysis (1-4 paragraphs) answering the legal questions. Be sure to state the common law, statutory, or procedural rule(s) applicable to the questions and apply the facts of your problem set to the rule(s). If the problem set does not contain sufficient facts for you to analyze the legal questions completely, identify the additional facts you would need to provide a complete answer.

Exercise 10.1
Developing and Executing a Research Plan

Name: _____   Due Date: _____

Professor: _____   Section: _____

Problem Set: _____

I.   Obtaining Preliminary Information

II.   Drafting a Preliminary Issue Statement

III.   Generating Search Terms

IV.   Planning and Executing Your Research Plan

    A.

B.

C.

D.

E.

F.

G.

H.

I.

J.

K.

V.   Answering the Legal Questions